B

GARDENING
FOR
FRAGRANCE

Jasminum polyanthum, which can be grown outside in mild gardens, is always a favourite indoor plant for its sweet fragrance, most powerful at night.

GARDENING
FOR
FRAGRANCE

Jane Taylor

WARD LOCK LIMITED · LONDON

ACKNOWLEDGEMENTS

The publishers are grateful to the following agencies/photographers for granting permission to reproduce the colour photographs: Harry Smith Horticultural Photographic Collection (front cover, pp. 2, 11, 27 (right), 43 (above right, below left, below right), 50 & 55); Photos Horticultural Picture Library (pp. 10, 15, 39 (below left, below right), 47, 51 & 59); John Glover (p. 27, left); Pat Brindley (pp. 31, 38 (above left), & 43 (above left)); and Peter McHoy (p. 39, above right).

All the line drawings are by Wendy Bramall.

House editor Denis Ingram

Text filmset in Bembo
by Hourds Typographica, Stafford

Printed and bound in Portugal
by Resopal

British Library Cataloguing in Publication Data

Taylor, Jane
Gardening for fragrance.
1. Gardens. Scented plants
I. Title   II. Series
635.9'68

ISBN 0-7063-6744-8

CONTENTS

Introduction 7

1   Getting the most from fragrant plants 9

2   Fragrant borders 14

3   In-and-out gardening with fragrant plants 21

4   The upper storey 26

5   Fragrant gardening for busy gardeners 36

6   Fragrance in the house 42

7   Touch and smell 48

8   The queen of flowers 53

9   Bringing them up to the nose 61

10   The scented conservatory 64

Appendices 68

Glossary of botanical names suggesting fragrance 93

Bibliography 94

Index 95

INTRODUCTION

Everyone who begins to plant and tend a garden works in three dimensions of space, and the fourth – time – in which all creatures on this earth are trapped. As land animals with the ability to see colour, and to see both far and wide, we are all too easily beguiled by bright flowers at the expense of other, more elusive but more haunting qualities. One of these is fragrance, which I like to think of as a fifth dimension in the garden. With its unique ability to evoke memories we thought lost for ever, to transport us in thought far from our actual surroundings, fragrance liberates the human psyche from its restrictive four dimensions of space and linear time.

The sense of smell is one that can be developed, just as surely as the sense of colour. Little children perceive only bright, primary colours; adults may learn to appreciate the subtlest of tones as well. But many people seem to remain little children where the sense of smell is concerned. I hope that after reading these pages, you will become – if you are not already – more aware of fragrance in the garden, of its permutations, of the resemblance of one scent to another.

You may have heard, or even voiced yourself, the opinion that plants do not smell as sweet as they used to. To the extent that this is true – and there is a grain of truth in it – it is perhaps the fault of that well-developed colour awareness of ours, combined with the greatly improved quality of colour illustrations which means that gardening books rely less and less on descriptions of flowers, and the fact that fragrance is notoriously difficult to describe at all. Please bear with me if, all too often, I have to fall back on phrases such as 'sweetly-scented', 'richly perfumed' or 'aromatic'. Whenever possible, I will liken a fragrance to something familiar – vanilla, almond, chocolate, apple – perfumes and scents known to all of us.

But the fact that there is no proper vocabulary for describing in non-scientific terms what something smells like does not mean that fragrance is not still very much with us. Sometimes, it is true, varieties of plants which have been bred for bigger, brighter flowers have lost part or all of their perfume in the process – the florists' cyclamen is one, and some new roses do not have much perfume. But the fragrance of the cyclamen is not truly lost, and now daintier varieties are being raised which smell deliciously sweet. And though not every modern rose smells sweet, plenty do; and plenty of old roses, often extolled for their fragrance, are in fact sadly lacking.

As well as looking out for fragrant varieties of familiar plants, you will, I hope, soon start to consider fragrant alternatives to well-known, unscented flowers. Thus in place of the cheerful, but unperfumed, yellow winter jasmine, *Jasminum nudiflorum*, you may turn to the subtler charms of spicy-scented witch hazel, *Hamamelis*, or of wintersweet, *Chimonanthus praecox*, of which the variety 'Luteus' is a clean, spring-fresh yellow in colour but as heartachingly sweet as the ordinary kind with translucent, ice-pale petals.

These fragrant alternatives are not necessarily any harder to grow than their soulless counterparts. Sometimes, it is true, they may be more expensive to buy, but that is partly a question of supply and demand. It is up to us gardeners to make fragrance as much a priority as the other qualities we appreciate: colour, beauty of leaf or of form, a long season of flower or the appeal of the old-fashioned. Nurserymen have to live like anyone else, and must be a little businesslike, though most survive on incomes which many people would regard as impossibly low. They stay in business because they love their plants; but they are obliged to produce the plants we, the buyers, want. If what we want are fragrant plants, then these will become available, and our gardens will be the richer for this fifth dimension.

CHAPTER 1

GETTING THE MOST FROM FRAGRANT PLANTS

Creating a fragrant garden is not simply a case of planting sweet-smelling flowers. By correct siting and cultivation, the value of fragrance from flowers and leaves can be greatly enhanced; by planting in the wrong place, much of the perfume may be lost.

THE IMPORTANCE OF SHELTER

The great enemy of gardens in many areas, and certainly the enemy of fragrance, is wind. A gentle breeze may waft perfume towards you; a blustery wind will be more likely to dissipate it entirely. So the first priority for a fragrant garden must be shelter. If you live in an area where strong winds are the norm, you may find it easier to create just one special sheltered corner in your garden for your fragrant plants. Gardens that are already somewhat sheltered by surrounding trees, walls, buildings, will offer greater scope.

Much can be done in windy gardens by planting dividing hedges and screens to make 'garden rooms' in which fragrance can be held captive. These sheltering screens themselves may be fragrant: honeysuckle (*Lonicera*) twining on a fence; a barrier of *Rosa rugosa* for its fragrant blooms or of the sweet briar, *R. rubiginosa*, for its apple-scented foliage; a shelter-belt of almond-scented *Salix triandra* or (space permitting) of the balsam poplar, *Populus balsamifera*. For a greater initial outlay you could construct sheltering walls, against which you could plant many fragrant plants, taking advantage of the extra warmth from the wall to grow less hardy plants: the Californian laurel, *Umbellularia californica*, for its heady, medicinal aroma; the Chilean jasmine, *Mandevilla suaveolens*, for its fragrant white flowers like huge periwinkles among neat dark foliage; the south African *Amaryllis belladonna*, a bulb bearing pink trumpets, smelling deliciously of ripe apricots, in late summer and early autumn. Or those walls could house a collection of fragrant climbing roses, a wisteria, a summer jasmine.

The cultivation of fragrant plants is no different from that of any other plant: give them the conditions they appreciate, and they in turn will give of their best. Most plants, whether trees, shrubs, climbers, bulbs,

Most camellias are unscented, but *C. sasanqua* 'Narumi Gata' has a sweet fragrance. It needs shelter to protect the flowers from frost damage.

perennials or annuals, will do best in soil that is thoroughly prepared by digging, incorporating as much as you can spare of well-rotted compost or manure, spent hops, leaf or bracken mould. This digging should be done in autumn for preference, leaving the soil bare for the winter so that frosts and rain can break down the clods. If you are making a new border where there has been grass, the grass can first be killed with herbicide and then dug in, the turfy top spit laid face down at the bottom of the trench on to which you will turn the next spit of soil. But you should be quite sure, whether taking in a formerly grassed area or digging over bare soil, that there are no perennial weeds remaining alive to infiltrate your new plantings. These days, with such a wide choice of effective herbicides, it is much easier to avoid the problem of surviving roots of bindweed or ground elder, nettle or dock, if you are cleaning a whole area before planting. If you are replanting a small area of an existing border, you may need to paint individual leaves of these pernicious weeds with herbicide, to avoid the risk of the chemical drifting on to plants you want to keep.

In spring, you can rake over your autumn-dug soil. On clay soils, a good dressing of coarse grit will help to improve drainage and make the soil easier to work; on sandy soils, you should be – for most plants at least – even more generous with the compost or other humus. Unfortunately, the most popular and easily-handled forms of humus, peat and ground bark, have virtually no food value for plants, so if you have to rely on these you should dress the soil in spring before planting with a good general fertilizer such as Growmore.

Heliotrope can be grown from seed each year; the best fragrance usually comes from the paler coloured kinds.

After planting, a mulch of peat or bark will help to retain moisture and suppress annual weeds, while those that do germinate will be very much easier to remove. Always put down a mulch on moist soil; if you apply it when the soil is dry, water will have difficulty penetrating. A cosy mulch will also help to keep the roots of the less hardy plants warm in winter.

Some plants, of course, have special requirements. As well as the question of sun or shade, certain plants have firm preferences in the matter of soil. Most Mediterranean plants, plants with silver foliage, and some bulbs, like sharply-drained soil in full sun, and would grow soft and sappy in enriched soil such as I have just described. Others – especially rhododendrons and azaleas, camellias, clethras and most magnolias – must have an acid soil to thrive. Fortunately for those who garden on sticky clay or on chalk, there are many plants that will do well in these conditions especially when the soil is improved with all the humus you can spare.

KEY SITES FOR FRAGRANT PLANTS

However much or little shelter you can contrive in your garden, there are certain key sites where you can concentrate your fragrant plants to get the most value from them. If you put sweet-smelling shrubs and plants around your door, then every time you go in or out you will be able to enjoy their fragrance. Cottage gardens often had a bush of lavender or lad's love (*Artemisia abrotanum*) by the door, or a tangle of jasmine or honeysuckle over the porch. If there is a window in your sitting room or bedroom which you often open in summer, then choose fragrant plants to grow nearby. A bedroom window could be wreathed with fragrant climbing roses or wisteria. A downstairs window with a border beneath it will give you scope for planting night-scented stocks, *Matthiola bicornis*, or tobacco flowers, *Nicotiana*, regal or Madonna lilies, blue petunias: all night-scented flowers to add enchantment to summer evenings by the open window.

On warmer evenings, and during sunny days, you may find time to sit out on your patio or in a special sitting corner of your garden. Here, too, fragrant plants can be concentrated. Patios are generally well-sheltered by house walls, and designed to catch plenty of sun. This makes them ideal places to plant sun-loving shrubs such as myrtle, *Myrtus communis*, which makes a rounded dome of dark green foliage covered, in late summer, in fuzzy, cream-white, sweet-scented flowers. It was for long a habit of brides to carry a sprig of myrtle in their wedding bouquet and to root it afterwards, planting the young cutting in just such a sheltered spot to remind them through their married lives of their wedding day.

A warm corner like this, too, would be the best place for lemon verbena and for the pineapple sage, both of which describe their fragrance in their names. Lemon verbena, *Aloysia triphylla*, is a shrub that is barely frost-tolerant, but easy to root from cuttings (Fig. 1). The pineapple sage,

Fig. 1 Many fragrant plants can be increased by softwood cuttings as easily as the familiar bedding geranium, shown here. Note where the cut is made and which buds and leaves are removed. Set the cuttings around the edge of a pot to root.

Salvia rutilans, which bears spires of crimson-scarlet flowers over its fresh green, fragrant foliage in late summer and autumn, is also tender, but will often grow again from the roots if cut down by frost.

In the garden of the house where I was born and brought up, there are two or three special sitting places, sheltered by walls and paved for warmth underfoot on sunny days. In one of these there has been for as long as I can remember a plant of the Mexican orange blossom, *Choisya ternata*. A handsome, glossy-leaved evergreen shrub with pungent foliage, this bears starry white fragrant flowers in spring and summer. Another is a little arbour, with a small wooden shelter covered in climbers: the thornless rose 'Zéphirine Drouhin', jasmine, honeysuckle, all twining in a tangle among the evergreen leaves of ivy, which render the whole edifice virtually waterproof.

An arbour can be more simply made with a wooden or metal trellis framework, or even a ready-made garden arch, set against a fence or wall perhaps to give a solid backing. This would be suitable only for dry days; but wet weather is not the best for fragrance anyway.

AIRBORNE FRAGRANCE

Sitting in your arbour or on your patio, you are going to be quite close to your fragrant flowers. And walking round the garden, it is no hardship to bend to inhale the fragrance of at least the taller plants. But some plants have the precious quality of releasing their perfume freely on the air. Such are the great climbing roses of the synstylae type, wild roses, and their nearly-related hybrids, characterized by huge swags of many tiny flowers at midsummer or later. In colour they are normally white, sometimes enhanced by yolk-yellow stamens; for fragrance they are unsurpassed. Honeysuckle is well-known for its airborne scent, especially strong at nightfall. In spring, beds of hyacinths are generous enough with their perfume to conquer even London rush-hour traffic at twenty paces. A big bush of tree lupin, *Lupinus arboreus*; *Philadelphus* or mock orange; a single spike even of regal, oriental or madonna lily; a lime tree in blossom; the resinous sun roses such as *Cistus ladanifer*: these are all plants that do not hold fast to their perfume, but freely give of it to anyone passing, filling the summer air. Stocks and pinks and heliotrope, tobacco plants and the incense plant, *Humea elegans*, add to the summer cocktail of scent, taking over from laburnum and wisteria and the honeysuckle azalea, *Rhododendron luteum*. Throughout the chapters to come, I will mention other plants with this precious characteristic, whether of flower or of leaf. They are especially worthy of cherishing in the fragrant garden.

CHAPTER 2

FRAGRANT BORDERS

Fragrant plants have their place in every kind of gardening, from the most formal and labour-intensive to the utterly relaxed and carefree. More and more people are coming to find that a rewarding compromise between the two extremes lies in the mixed-border style of gardening.

The mixed border, as its name implies, includes all sorts of components: shrubs, perennials, bulbs, annuals and biennials, and possibly a tree or two and some climbers. This willingness to mix different kinds of plants frees the gardener from many constraints, and opens the way to a host of associations in which each plant's special qualities can be enhanced by its neighbours.

As the main components of most mixed borders will be shrubs, perennials and bulbs, I will concentrate on these for the time being. For all that, bedding plants, climbers and trees may creep into this chapter, just as they will into your mixed borders.

Often the most pleasing schemes are made by choosing plants in a fairly narrow colour range. This may be a harmonious grouping of colours chosen from the same band of the spectrum. Or we may choose contrasts of colour, which will generally be easier to handle if two, or perhaps at most three, contrasting colours are chosen. Though I don't want to suggest that one should choose a visually inferior plant just for the sake of its fragrance, I think there is a very real tendency when planning plant groups to think first in terms of colour and perhaps of shape, with fragrance well down the list of considerations. This is surely a waste of one of the most evocative qualities a garden can offer. Let's see how this might work out in practice, by planning some specific groups based on a definite colour scheme but with fragrance a major factor in the selection of material.

ACCENT ON YELLOW WITH
YEAR-ROUND SCENT

First, a group for year-round effect, perhaps in a key position in a mixed border where it can be seen at all times. The colour theme is green and

Rhododendron luteum is known as the honeysuckle azalea because of its strong, sweet perfume.

yellow: shades of yellow in flower from cream to canary, and of green in foliage from lime to blackish-green, avoiding any blue-toned leaves. Evergreen foliage must form the core of a year-round group, so let us start with an *Elaeagnus* with gold and green variegated leaves, which many people already have in their gardens. If you are starting from scratch, 'Limelight' is an especially good kind; all have tiny, but sweetly scented, silvery cream flowers in autumn. Give it plenty of space, cut out any shoots that revert to green, and don't be afraid to cut branches for the house or to keep the shrub in shape and in bounds. Later, in winter, *Mahonia japonica* will contribute a lily-of-the-valley perfume from its gracefully arching flower sprays composed of small yellow bells. This is a fair-sized, rounded shrub with bold evergreen, somewhat holly-like foliage. Mahonias were formerly called berberis and, space permitting, you could include one of the true berberis as the last sizeable evergreen shrub in this group. *B. sargentiana* has small lemon-yellow flowers wafting a powerful scent of honey on the spring air.

Our evergreen backbone planted, it's time to add more flower and fragrance. For spring, plant yellow *Crocus chrysanthus* and, to follow, scented narcissi such as 'Yellow Cheerfulness'. For late spring, if your soil is suitable for azaleas, the old honeysuckle azalea (botanically called *Rhododendron luteum*) is as delectably perfumed as its English name implies. It adds the bonus of rich crimson and flame autumn foliage. Instead, or as well if you've space, the shrub rose 'Frühlingsgold' gives off a sweet spicy scent from its wide yellow single flowers in late spring. And while you are waiting for some of the slower-growing shrubs, such as the mahonia, to bulk up, you could add a tree lupin, *Lupinus arboreus*, fast-growing and short-lived, but treasured for the sweet bean-field scent of its clear yellow spikes at midsummer borne on a rounded, fresh green shrub. Against the darkish green of the berberis and mahonia the golden-leaved mock orange, *Philadelphus coronarius* 'Aureus', will show to advantage. Its creamy flowers are borne at midsummer and will take over the role of the azalea in filling the air with fragrance.

It is time to add some herbaceous plants to a largely shrubby group. Some of the best for this colour range are the day lilies (Fig. 2), starting with the so-called lemon lily, *Hemerocallis flava*, in early summer. The later-flowering kinds come in many colours, but again it is the yellows which have the sweetest fragrance. Reliable kinds are 'Hyperion', 'Marion Vaughn' and the lovely pale 'Whichford', all with trumpet-shaped blooms. Day lilies have another bonus for the mixed border too; their new foliage as it spears through is the freshest of greens, the very essence of spring. They are much easier to grow, too, than the true lilies which develop a scaly bulb with fleshy roots: these need a rich soil with good

Fig. 2 The most fragrant day lilies (*Hemerocallis*) are those with yellow flowers.

Fig. 3 In a border group of yellow flowers, tree lupins (*Lupinus arboreus*) and daylilies give fragrance; they are set off by the bold dark foliage of *Helleborus foetidus*.

drainage, and shelter from spring frosts on the young foliage. A position among shrubs suits lilies well, so we could add to our group a few bulbs of one of the easiest to grow, *Lilium regale* 'Royal Gold', the yellow variety of the regal lily with the same generous, free-floating scent.

Contrasting with the fresh green spears of the day lilies, *Helleborus foetidus* has handsome darkest green long-fingered foliage. This plant is unjustly called the stinking hellebore, for the flowers of some forms are very sweetly perfumed with a fragrance that hangs in the winter air. The little green bells are borne in stemmy clusters above the dark green fans of foliage. Only if you bruise them will you catch a whiff of the smell that gave the plant its botanical and English names (Fig. 3).

COOL SHADES FOR SUMMER FRAGRANCE

Sometimes a plant group making a concentrated impact over a short season may be what is needed. In summer a group based on pinks, mauves and purples, with grey and glaucous foliage, can give a welcome cool note that would seem merely chilly in winter. Let's take as centre-piece for such a group a shrub rose: perhaps lilac-pink 'Louise Odier' or mauve 'Reine des Violettes', both fragrant Bourbon roses with the flat-faced, quartered, old-fashioned style of flower and a second season of bloom.

With their domesticated appearance these roses assort well with other cottagey plants: lavender and purple-leaved sage – *Salvia officinalis* 'Purpurascens' – which is a soft grey-purple, not the harsher coppery-maroon usually implied; pinks (*Dianthus*) for their clove scent and bearded irises for their sword-like leaves. *Iris pallida dalmatica* has the best foliage, broad and glaucous to echo the blue-grey foliage of the pinks; its classic fleur-de-lis, pale lavender-blue flowers are fragrant too. This is a group that will demand full sun and a well-drained soil, with extra feeding for the rose. To add still more fragrance, another mock orange, plain green-leaved this time: *Philadelphus* 'Belle Etoile' has squarish flowers, white with a purple stain at their hearts, and a rich pineapple scent.

The season of this midsummer group can be extended by adding a lilac for late spring: *Syringa microphylla* 'Superba' is a good choice, for it has neat little leaves, is of fairly modest growth and often bears its rose-pink, fragrant spikes from late spring till autumn. Then, for more silvery foliage, I'd want to add *Buddleia* 'Lochinch', very grey in leaf and bearing stout lavender spikes well endowed with the honey fragrance of all the butterfly bushes. Spearing up among the lower plants, *Verbena bonariensis* adds another note of perfume from its little purple flowers borne in flat heads on branching, almost leafless stems.

OFFBEAT TONES AND WARM PERFUMES

The colour of foliage usually called 'purple' is generally a coppery-maroon that assorts as well with the colours of this group as it does with yellows and reds. In its less strident manifestations this dark-pigmented foliage also makes the ideal background for buffs and browns, apricots and creams, an unusual colour-range that deserves careful handling. A purple *Cotinus* such as 'Royal Purple', or a berberis of similar colouring, is a suitable, but scentless, background against which we can set softly toned fragrant flowers.

The hybrid musk roses are among the best of shrub roses, sturdy and tough, with a tremendous display in summer and autumn and a rich perfume. Two varieties belong in this group: 'Moonlight' for its creamy flowers and chocolate-coloured young growths, and 'Buff Beauty' with flowers of apricot, honey and cream opening from flame buds. Of similar honey-gold and buff-apricot colouring is *Buddleia × weyeriana* 'Golden Glow': its flower spikes are formed of rounded heads of decreasing size, rather than the solid tapering spikes of the more familiar butterfly bushes, but it has all their warm perfume.

The white *Lilium regale* deserves a space here, for its petals are backed with mahogany to echo the brown tones we need. Other true lilies to try are the African Queen strain in pure apricot-yellow, or the rare, expensive and utterly desirable *L. × testaceum*. A small-flowered, especially sweet-scented day lily called *Hemerocallis* 'Golden Chimes' demands inclusion too, for its warm yellow flowers are backed with copper.

The scent of lilies is most powerful at dusk, and so is honeysuckle. The late Dutch honeysuckle, *Lonicera periclymenum* 'Serotina', has enough mahogany-red on its creamy petals to qualify for a place in this group, tethered to a stout pole perhaps to give height. The clove-like scent of wallflowers (*Cheiranthus cheiri*), earlier in the year, is always welcome, and there are several cinnamon and tan shades to choose from. Earlier still, *Crocus chrysanthus* has brown-backed kinds such as 'Gipsy Girl'. Though you must bend to catch it, the scent of these little crocuses is very like 'Joy', once said to be the most expensive perfume in the world.

Bronze fennel, *Foeniculum vulgare* 'Purpureum', needs touching to release its aniseed aroma, but stroking its young growths, like soft brown foxes' brushes, is no hardship. And although they have no scent, it is tempting to include cream and coral kniphofias (they can hardly be called red hot pokers when they are not red) and the bronze-leaved, tangerine-flowered montbretia which you will find in the catalogues as *Crocosmia* 'Solfatare'. Both the pokers and the montbretia flower in summer.

The dahlia-like *Cosmos atrosanguineus* is a must in this buff, apricot and brown group. Until recently quite scarce, it has now quickly earned the nicknames 'chocolate plant' or 'cocoa plant'. This is not just for its rich, dark colouring, of deepest maroon. When you bend to the flower, you find that its scent is exactly that of a hot cup of cocoa. It is a good deal more frost-resistant than dahlias, although it dies down entirely for the winter. But it has the reputation of tenderness. I believe that this is because it does not start into visible new growth until early summer each year. Faced with what looks like an empty patch of soil in the border, many gardeners either forget what was there and plant something new in spring; or decide, by late spring, that their cosmos is dead, and then plant some other plant on top of it. Either course is usually fatal; your fork spears the tubers of the cosmos and it gives up the struggle. Be patient, and nine years out of ten it will reward you by pushing up new shoots and finally those deep chocolate, single flowers on knee-high stems.

A SHADE DRAMATIC

A purple and gold group is something else again, dramatic but perhaps not always easy to live with. Start with a backbone of purple and lime-yellow foliage: the *Cotinus* already proposed, or *Berberis* × *ottawensis* 'Superba' perhaps, with *Robinia pseudoacacia* 'Frisia' or our old friend the golden mock orange for summer perfume. Add pale yellow rose 'Frühlingsgold' for late spring fragrance, and follow on into summer with a dark crimson – purple one. For later summer make byzantine mixtures of colour, purple and scarlet, ochre and magenta. For fragrance in this range of colour plant some brightly coloured phloxes: they can be had in rich purple and wine crimson, as well as hot red. It is a fact of nature, however, that the most fragrant flowers are of pale colouring. There are exceptions – crimson roses, for example (though not even all of those) or the strong magenta of *Rosa rugosa* 'Roseraie de l'Hay', which would fit well in this group, especially as its autumn foliage is corn-gold. Next after the pale colours for scent come purple and violet; there is least among hot orange and deep yellow. Strangely, however, some orange tulips are fragrant: 'De Wet', 'Orange Parrot', and some others. How helpful it would be if all bulb merchants told us, in their catalogues, which kinds were scented.

CHAPTER 3

IN-AND-OUT GARDENING WITH FRAGRANT PLANTS

I've suggested that one of the reasons fragrance became less important in our gardens was the development of high-quality colour photography. At an earlier period, during the last century, interest in fragrance also suffered a temporary decline, eclipsed by a fascination with colour – manifested in carpet bedding – and with exotic plants. During the Victorian era, cheap coal, cheap labour and developments in the techniques of glass-making combined to bring hothouses within the reach of almost every gardener. At about the same time a host of new plants were introduced from tropical and subtropical areas. These novelties were raised in the new glasshouses and used in the bedding schemes of the day.

We still see the legacy of this fashion in many of today's gardens, where scarlet salvias, blue lobelias, orange and yellow marigolds are planted to form bright but scentless patterns. Here I want to write about some of the bedding plants that you could use either in formal schemes, or informally among your mixed border plants, to enjoy yet more fragrance, as well as colour, in your garden.

ANNUALS, BIENNIALS, TENDERS AND EPHEMERALS

An annual that has lost none of its popularity is the sweet pea, *Lathyrus odoratus*, which earned its English name from its cherished fragrance. Unfortunately, in the pursuit of larger, frillier or brighter flowers, the breeders of sweet peas have sometimes sacrificed perfume: the showier kinds often have the least scent. You can be fairly sure that if the seed catalogue doesn't mention scent in the description of a given variety, it will have been at least partly bred out. The best new kinds for fragrance are indicated in the catalogues, but I want to suggest you also try the old-fashioned kinds offered by one or two seedsmen. Sometimes you may find them noted simply as 'old-fashioned', or described as the original Spencer type, perhaps. Other catalogues go further back in time even than this, to offer varieties very close in character to the original wild sweet pea: 'Matucana' and 'Quito', both maroon and purple, or 'Painted

Fig. 4 Sweet pea seeds can be sown in a pot in autumn or in spring.

Lady' in rose-pink and white. The flowers are smaller than those of the
new kinds, but the scent is unsurpassed.

Sweet peas are not difficult to grow if you give them rich soil. They
can be sown in spring or in autumn; the big seeds can be sown in a pot
(Fig. 4). Give them some warmth to encourage germination if you sow
early in spring; keep autumn-sown seedlings in a cold-frame and plant
out in mid-spring when the soil is warming up.

You may want to grow sweet peas only for cutting; if so, a row
among the vegetables is the answer. But in a garden setting there are
many possibilities. The new low-growing strains – Snoopea, or pink-
and-white Cupid – make dense little plants that can be used among roses
old and new (with an eye to colour clashes). Taller kinds can be planted
in a group of five or seven on a wigwam of canes in a border.

A lowly bedding plant that remains popular today, probably as much
for its scent as for any other quality, is sweet alyssum, *Alyssum maritimum*.
Used in generous drifts it will fill the garden air with its honey scent all
summer. As it comes in white and shades of rose, mauve and purple, you
could use it informally in the pink and mauve planting I wrote about in
the previous chapter, grouped around a lilac-toned old-fashioned rose.
Your sweet alyssum could be planted in drifts among the shrubs and herbaceous plants, filling any gaps to the front of the border.

In the same sort of colour range, but with more sparkle to their tones, and including pure pink, bright scarlet and violet, are the bedding verbenas. As well as the varieties raised from seed, which are not always the most fragrant, there are some named kinds which you can keep going by taking cuttings every autumn. Most of these, but not the scarlet kinds, are deliciously scented: cherry red 'Lawrence Johnston', bright violet 'Loveliness', and two-tone candy pink 'Silver Ann' and 'Pink Bouquet'. These varieties tend also to have a more spreading habit than the seed strains, so fewer plants will be needed. Try a group of 'Pink Bouquet' frothing around the base of one of the new, red- or pink-variegated phormiums (Fig. 5). Of taller habit, suitable for planting further back in the border, is *Verbena venosa* with insistent violet-mauve flowers.

Fig. 5 The bold foliage of a red and purple leaved phormium looks dramatic above pale pink *Verbena* 'Pink Bouquet'.

SORTING OUT STOCKS

Verbenas are just one of the plants we frequently grow as annuals, but which are in truth tender perennials; *V. venosa* indeed is pretty hardy in mild areas at least. Stocks, too: sometimes in cottage gardens where the climate is not too severe and the plants are not uprooted after flowering they go on year after year, becoming almost woody at the base. Usually, though, they are grown as annuals or biennials. Stocks are confusing plants; or at least the names seedsmen give to the various strains are puzzling. Full marks to Thompson & Morgan for simplifying stocks: 'if you are sowing in spring for summer flowers any variety with "HHA" will be suitable. If you require them for spring flowering choose from the varieties prefixed "HB".'

Beauty of Nice or Mammoth are among the kinds classed as HHA – half-hardy annual – which can be sown in spring: not too early (*pace* T & M) or they will get starved in their trays instead of making nice bushy plants. Wait until mid-spring to sow them, without artificial heat; prick them off into pots (not trays); and you will have strong plants to set out at midsummer. They will give you flower, and that warm clove fragrance, until early autumn. These kinds are bigger and more interesting than the ten-week stocks, and come in a wider range of colours. Both can be had in double-flowered kinds which you can select when they are still tiny: just prick out the pale green seedlings and discard the dark green, which will be single-flowered. Whether single or double, stocks come in jewel colours of carmine, ruby, amethyst and rose, pure white, and an alluring creamy primrose.

The well-known Brompton stocks are biennials, sown in high summer to flower the following spring. In light (but not starved) soils and mild gardens you can plant them out in autumn, but if you garden on cold sticky clay soil in a frost pocket then you will succeed better with them if you pot them for the winter and keep them in a frame, preferably with a little heat from a soil-warming cable, or in your glasshouse. When that heavy clove perfume greets your nose in spring all that effort – which isn't so very extreme, after all – seems worth it.

PLAIN OR MIXED: FAVOURITE BIENNIALS

Many biennials are sown earlier than Brompton stocks, to give them time to make sturdy plants before autumn. Such are sweet williams, *Dianthus barbatus*, classic cottage flowers, cherished for their fragrance and their rich Persian-carpet colours. Sweet williams are a bit of trouble to grow well, it's true. Sow them early, in boxes in mid-spring; prick out the seedlings and then, when large enough, line them out in a spare corner of the vegetable garden until, in autumn, you plant them where they are to flower. Sow them any later and they won't flower so freely.

Mixtures of sweet williams are fine for fragrance, but for visual effect plantings of a single colour, or two symmetrically arranged perhaps, will be more satisfying. Once over, they can be ripped up to make way for an annual that you have sown later than usual to hold it back – in late spring or even early summer. Nasturtiums (*Tropaeolum majus*) would do well in this role; they can be sown in pots, singly, and planted out to fill within days the empty space left by the sweet williams. The Gleam strain of nasturtiums is especially sweet-scented.

Another well-loved biennial, which you can raise yourself from seed or buy as young plants, is the wallflower. Many wallflower seeds, and most young plants, are offered as mixtures only. If you care about planning colour schemes as well as fragrance you may want to choose individual colours, mixing dramatic scarlet wallflowers with primrose or white tulips, perhaps, or ruby-crimson with pink tulips and forget-me-nots of clear blue. This will mean raising your own seedlings. Sow in the open ground at the point when spring turns to summer, just as you are throwing out last year's plants. Prick out the seedlings in lines, and finally bed them out, in generous quantities, in autumn. If you plant a bed of them beneath a window, and it should happen while they are flowering in spring to be warm enough to open that window, the perfume will waft in.

If stocks, sweet williams, even wallflowers are a bit of a fiddle to grow well, there are other, undemanding annuals and biennials to bring scent to our gardens. I've already mentioned nasturtiums and sweet alyssum. In the stock family are the little Virginian stocks, coloured lilac, carmine and white, quick to flower, full of perfume and easy to grow. Drop a few seeds in the cracks among the paving stones of your patio, or give a packet to your children to give them the taste for fragrant flowers at an early age.

Asperula setosa is the annual woodruff with blue flowers on a low-growing plant, another candidate for popping in among the cracks of paving to add fragrance to a sitting-place or to drift among taller plants.

Much taller than these lowly annuals, but no harder to grow, are the annual lupins. They come in various colours: yellow *Lupinus luteus*, blue *L. hartwegii* or the very variable *L. mutabilis*, with a botanical name indicating its changeable character. All are deliciously fragrant, with that warm bean-field aroma so characteristic of flowers in the pea family. Bulkier annuals such as these are invaluable for filling gaps in the border, perhaps where the previous occupant has died from frost or drought or debility. Lupins, being members of the pea family, also have the extra quality of feeding the soil where they grow, by means of the nitrogen-fixing nodules on their roots.

CHAPTER 4

THE UPPER STOREY

Think for a moment, if you will, of the way plants grow in the wild. The detail, the exact species, will of course depend on the part of the world in question. But the basic principles are the same: an upper storey of trees, an understorey – where light levels permit – of shrubs and herbaceous plants; bulbs spearing up from under ground to flower before the deciduous tree canopy comes into leaf, or – in dry climates – blooming after the rains; and climbers, the opportunists of the plant world, using shrubs and trees as supports on which to hoist themselves towards the light.

Adapting this principle to the domestic scene gives a relaxed style of gardening which will permit you to grow more plants in a given space, and to grow them in a fashion which is close to nature's way. And more plants, if you choose aright, mean more fragrance. It is easy to forget that flowering trees can bring scent to the garden just as surely as plants that are nearer to the nose. And though everyone knows the fragrance of honeysuckle (Fig. 6) and jasmine, there are other sweet-smelling climbers that can both decorate and perfume your garden.

Fig. 6 Honeysuckle may strangle a living host; to be safe, give it a support such as this timber structure.

Left: The almond-scented white flowers of *Prunus yedoensis* are set off by crimson calyces. *Right:* Most eucryphias make narrow, columnar evergreen trees. 'Rostrevor' is one of the best.

SCENT FROM FRAGRANT CLIMBERS AND TREES

Cherries and crabs are widely planted spring-flowering trees, usually chosen for their showy qualities rather than their fragrance. Yet there are scented varieties of both. Why choose the overplanted, ungainly and crudely coloured cherry 'Kanzan' when you could have almond-scented, white 'Jo-nioi'? Or, if you want to take a chance with the weather causing frost-damage to the flowers, the graceful, early-flowering *Prunus* × *yedoensis* bears clouds of almond-scented blush-white flowers on arching branches.

If spring frosts are a regular problem in your area, a late-flowering crab may be a safer choice. You could select *Malus coronaria* 'Charlottae', its double shell-pink flowers scented of violets, opening in late spring and early summer. Earlier than this, but still late enough to escape most damaging frosts, is 'Profusion', best, and among the sweetest, of the purple-leaved crabs with wine-crimson flowers. These dark-leaved crabs need careful placing in the garden. In informal surroundings, especially, they tend to look uncomfortably artificial, making a heavy indigestible lump of dark colour in the landscape. One of the most satisfactory ways to grow them, in a frankly urban or suburban setting, is in company with other coloured leaves in place of the more usual green: a purple crab and a silver weeping pear, *Pyrus salicifolia* 'Pendula', or purple with the fresh lime-yellow of *Robinia pseudoacacia* 'Frisia'.

The first pair could well be used in a border to add height, bulk and early interest to the pink, purple and grey-leaved group described in Chapter 2. The crab will open the season of fragrance and flower.

EVERYMAN'S MAGNOLIAS

It may be that you want a more aristocratic tree than a cherry or a crab. If so, you could choose a magnolia. There are magnolias to flower from early spring to late summer; many of them are wonderfully fragrant. And there is no need to be put off by their reputation of being difficult to grow; there is at least one magnolia for any garden, whether on chalk soil or peat, sand or clay. Magnolias have fleshy roots which are prone to rotting if damaged, especially if newly planted in cold soil with the winter dormant season ahead. Plant your magnolia in spring, in soil that is warming up, and into which you have incorporated all the humus you can. Well-rotted compost or manure, peat, spent hops, leaf mould, bracken mould: all these will help your magnolia to become established, and will nourish it as it grows. Such attentions are especially necessary on sticky clay or hungry sand. Once you have planted your magnolia, you should never hoe around it, for the roots are near the surface and are easily damaged. Instead, a loose mulch of leaves or bracken will keep the roots cool, nourish the tree and help to keep weeds at bay.

If spring frosts are not a threat in your area, and you are patient, then *Magnolia denudata*, the Chinese yulan, may be for you. Here is a small tree of great beauty when displaying its pure white, chalice-shaped flowers on bare branches. The yulan is a parent of everyman's magnolia, the Soulangiana hybrids, all of which have white flowers more or less stained with purple and equally liable to be caught by frosts. Prettier than these is the easy-going *M. × loebneri* 'Merrill', with starry, fragrant white flowers which it derives partly from one parent, the shrubby star magnolia, *M. stellata*. All the pink-flowered magnolias are exquisite and rather more demanding. For fragrance, seek out *M. sprengeri diva*; its chalice-shaped rich pink flowers appear, like those of all these kinds, too early to be safe from spring frosts.

When the gamble comes off, and the flowers are spared, all these early magnolias are handsome; some are breathtakingly beautiful. The finer they are – the yulan, the pink asiatics especially – the less they need an elaborate supporting cast. The simpler the planting scheme, the better.

But you should emphatically not carry simplicity to the extent of using them as lawn specimens with grass right to their very feet; for the competition for nutrients will starve and stunt the magnolia. Always keep a clear space around them, well mulched. A simple background of dark evergreen foliage for the white-flowered kinds, or of blue sky for the pink, will suffice. If you plan other flowering groups within the line of vision, do remember the purplish stain on the Soulangiana hybrids; it can clash horribly with the yellows and oranges of spring, to the detriment of both.

For many gardeners one of the summer-flowering magnolias may be a better choice. There is a group of them, all similar, but differing in cultural needs: which means that there is one for almost any garden. Their flowers are nodding bowls in place of the upright chalices of the spring-flowering kinds. These wide, white, sweetly fragrant blooms are enhanced by a great central boss of crimson. Most ordinary soils, well laced with humus, will grow *M. wilsonii* or *M. sinensis*. On acid soils, where rhododendrons and azaleas thrive, *M. sieboldii* is most suitable. At the other extreme, on chalk, plant *M. × highdownensis*. This hybrid actually originated in the Sussex garden of Highdown which was created in a chalk quarry, so its credentials as chalk-tolerant cannot be in doubt. All four make large shrubs or small trees, and grow remarkably fast when not starved of nourishment. All are blessed with a far-carrying fragrance and can well be planted behind lower-growing plants that will give flower and fragrance earlier or later in the year.

The north American evergreen *Magnolia grandiflora* flowers in late summer and even into autumn. It can be trained as a wall shrub – but give it plenty of space to grow sideways and outwards – or allowed to form a small free-standing tree. This it will do both in mild areas, and in those with not too fierce Continental climates, where a good summer ripening from ample sunshine compensates for frosty winters. 'Maryland' is a good new kind, perhaps a hybrid, which flowers at a young age; so do the older kinds 'Exmouth' and 'Goliath'. But seed-raised trees may keep you waiting many years for their creamy, richly lemon-scented, bowl-shaped flowers. The glossy evergreen foliage is handsome, but we want flowers, too, on our magnolias. In warm climates, as it might be in southern California, *M. grandiflora* may start to flower in late spring; the perfume at all seasons is intoxicating.

Although I have given much space to magnolias, this is still only a small selection of the kinds available to gardeners in temperate climes. There is no other group of hardy flowering trees that can hold a candle to them for beauty and fragrance. But this isn't to say that other scented or aromatic trees are unworthy of our notice.

The balsam poplars, fast-growing, easy but greedy trees, have foliage with a marked balsam scent. *Populus balsamifera* is one; the variegated *P. × candicans* 'Aurora' another. This is so boldly variegated with cream and pink that from a little distance the tree seems to be full of flower. Unpruned trees come green into leaf and take their colours later in the year; hard-pruned, or pollarded like a willow, they do the very reverse. In either case the balsam aroma is sometimes elusive, sometimes freely borne on the air. These arc trees for the impatient gardener. Just stick a sizeable cutting, 60–80cm (two feet or more) long, into the ground where you want your tree, and nine times out of ten it will take root and grow. But on no account put it near your house, for the far-reaching, greedy roots can damage foundations and drains.

Poplars, even hard-pruned, are not for small gardens. By contrast almost every garden-owner, given a suitably mild climate, could accommodate a eucryphia. These evergreens from the southern hemisphere form narrow, columnar trees decked in late summer with bowl-shaped white flowers filled with a brush of white, pink-tipped stamens and blessed with a delicate scent. The eucryphia most commonly offered is *E.* 'Nymansay', but if you can find it, *E. × intermedia* 'Rostrevor' is a fine thing, ideally suited to making a firm vertical accent in the garden landscape.

HOST TREES FOR FRAGRANT CLIMBERS

In a tree such as a eucryphia a climber might not be an appropriate feature; that slender outline is best left untrammelled. But often the support for a climber will be a tree or sizeable shrub, as it would be in nature. Say you have a full-grown hawthorn, or an old apple tree, unproductive but picturesque when full of fragrant blossom in spring. Rather than cut it down, you could well give it a second season of value by allowing it to host a climbing rose, a honeysuckle perhaps, or a scented clematis. A large tree – even a pine – could hold a wisteria, or one of the vigorous climbing roses in the synstylae group, of which the massive 'Kiftsgate' is the most famous. Even sweeter, with a far-reaching fruity perfume, are others in this group of climbing roses: 'Bobbie James', 'Rambling Rector', 'Polyantha Grandiflora'. Most of them are creamy white, with more or less pronounced yolk-yellow stamens; 'Paul's Himalayan Musk' is lilac-pink and 'Treasure Trove' apricot with mahogany young growths. All have wide clusters of many small flowers.

When you plant any climber to grow into a tree, remember that the roots of the tree will take much of the nourishment from the soil. This won't hurt a wisteria much – the richer the soil, the less they flower,

The strong-growing *Clematis rehderiana* bears its cowslip-scented flowers in autumn.

anyway. But roses, clematis, even honeysuckles, need good living. Plant them, then, far enough from the tree to stay beyond the reach of the main root system. A long cane, or a rope, can lead the climber into the tree; once there, and established, its own stems will keep it in place. A little judicious guidance with a forked pole will push long new shoots in the right direction. Let the wind be your ally, too; plant on the side of the prevailing wind if you can, so gales will push the climber more firmly into the tree instead of tearing it out.

WALLS AND STRUCTURES FOR
SCENTED CLIMBERS

Trees, of course, are not the only support for climbers. Most gardeners think first of walls for their climbers; and unless you live in an architectural gem which should on no account be concealed, where better to begin than the walls of your house? Then, of course, there are the walls of outhouses, garages, sheds; and you may even be fortunate enough to have a walled garden. All walls will need to be provided with support for climbers, few of which are self-clinging. Wires fixed to the wall with

Fig. 7 Support for fragrant climbers may range from a simple tripod to an elaborate pergola.

vine-eyes, wooden trellis securely bolted on, or even at a pinch plastic-covered trellised wire (available in brown, green or white) can all be used. Make sure the fixings are secure, or a night of rain and gales may bring the whole structure to the ground, and its climber with it. Most climbers can be grown on walls, but it makes sense to use the space for the choicest climbers and those that flower best with extra warmth. Some climbers prefer walls not in full, baking sun – especially the honeysuckles. Some roses, too, are happy on north walls: white, scented 'Madame Alfred Carrière' or the sumptuous, buff-yellow 'Gloire de Dijon' among them.

Climbers can equally well be grown on fences, and if you have an ugly wire fence, say, vigorous fragrant climbers such as *Lonicera japonica*, the

Fig. 8 Sweet peas can deck the uprights of a pergola, with a fragrant rose wreathing the crossbeams.

Japanese honeysuckle, or strong rambler roses, can conceal it. For spring another choice could be a fragrant form of *Clematis montana*, such as pale pink 'Elizabeth' with a pleasing vanilla scent. More elegant fences can be partly decked with more restrained climbers; solid larch-lap fencing can give something of the shelter of a wall.

Structures such as pergolas, arches and trellis screens can be architecturally handsome in their own right, or mere supports for climbers, best concealed as fast as possible (Fig. 7). Pergolas look best without too many different climbers. A simple scheme of wisteria for the cross-members, and a rose such as 'Aloha' with rich pink, sweetly-scented double flowers, for the uprights, will give fragrance and a succession of flowers with an unfussy look. On a large pergola one of the big rambling roses of the

'Kiftsgate' type, already mentioned, could be used, with pillar roses or sweet peas for the uprights (Fig. 8). A bush of lavender at the base of each upright would bring another note of perfume to the scheme.

Arches or a trellis panel will generally call for a single planting scheme, unless you construct a series of arches, which will almost amount to a pergola. As such structures are likely to be quite a feature in the garden, it is a good idea to add plants that will make up for the one deficiency of most fragrant climbers: their foliage. Say you wanted to make a scheme of soft pinks, mauves and blues on a panel of trellis dividing one part of your garden from the next, or to decorate an arch over a pathway. The fragrant, shell-pink perpetual-flowering rambler rose 'New Dawn' would combine prettily with pale blue-mauve *Clematis* 'Mrs Cholmon-dely', and you could add a group of shrubs to shade the roots of the clematis and add foliage and flower colour. *Potentilla* 'Royal Flush' and 'Princess' both have pink flowers and look good with *Berberis thunbergii* 'Rose Glow', its foliage variegated pink, cream and purple. In dry sunny sites *Ruta graveolens* 'Jackman's Blue' would add prettily divided glaucous blue foliage, and the front row could be occupied by grey-leaved, pink-flowered rock roses such as *Helianthemum* 'Wisley Pink'. In such a site the soil for the rose and the clematis would need extra careful preparation, and both climbers would benefit from annual mulching. In moister, richer soils, grow *Hosta sieboldiana* 'Elegans' for its large, glaucous blue leaves. *Lilium regale* would add rich perfume and white flowers in summer and would benefit from the shelter of the shrubs against late spring frosts (Fig. 9).

A special kind of garden construction is the arbour, where you sit when the weather permits. The arbour, more than any other part of the garden, should be bathed in perfume, and scented climbers can play their part. Fragrant living porches can be made from climbers such as jasmine or honeysuckle, too; but avoid roses, which snag people with their prickly stems. A possible exception is the sugar-pink double, perpetual-flowering rose 'Zéphirine Drouhin', which has as rich a perfume as any; but it does not lend itself so well as a twining climber to forming a covered porch.

In borders, extra height and colour can be obtained in a restricted space by growing climbers up poles or on tripods. A tripod can be a simple construction of bamboos designed to take sweet peas for one summer, or something more elaborate for a permanent climber such as a rose or a jasmine. A pole can be an ideal support, if strong and well secured in the ground, for a honeysuckle; these lovely climbers do tend to strangle host shrubs or trees. An imaginative use of honeysuckle I once saw had the climber growing on the bracing wire of a telephone pole which was

Fig. 9 Make a feature of a garden arch, with rose 'New Dawn' for summer-long flower, *Lilium regale* and bold hostas.

stuck, as they sometimes are, in someone's garden with no regard for aesthetics. The honeysuckle not only wreathed the wire so as to conceal it with a flowery mass, but also saved the unwary from tripping over it.

Another way of growing climbers will not save you any ground-space, but it may save you some weeding instead. For plenty of climbers can be allowed simply to flop about on the ground, perhaps given a little encouragement with peasticks driven in and half-snapped to lie horizon-tally, when the climber will make respectable ground cover, or disguise old stumps. Such cover can be much more effective than what garden centres sell as ground cover, for while the climber is thickening up, it can be gently lifted for you to weed underneath. But roses as ground cover are not, generally, much use; they never grow really thick, so weeds still germinate, and the stems of the rose are abominably prickly to weed around and through.

CHAPTER 5

FRAGRANT GARDENING FOR BUSY GARDENERS

All gardening involves some effort; there's no escaping it. But the amount of time available to people to care for their gardens differs, of course. It makes sense to choose a style of gardening that fits in with the time you have at your disposal and the effort you are prepared to put in.

FRAGRANCE FOR COMMUTERS

Those who have a long working day, or who spend hours a day commuting, are probably too tired to think of gardening in the evenings. What they need is a garden to relax in, not to worry over; a garden with fragrance on the air and flowers that show up at dusk. And they need to achieve this without spending every daylight hour of the weekend at work in the garden.

The colour that shows up best at dusk is white, with other pale colours – primrose, ice blue, blush pink – and silvery foliage almost as visible. Remembering, too, that many plants are most fragrant at night, you could plant an evening garden to soothe and enchant your weary senses.

Before the onset of Summer Time, the evenings will be too dark, and probably too cold, to tempt you into the garden. So at this season your evening plants should be close at hand. Late winter is the chief season of *Daphne odora* 'Aureomarginata', a small shrub of 1 m (3 ft) or so, with clusters of white flowers, purple-pink outside, and the characteristic spicy-sweet daphne perfume. Following it in spring, *D. pontica* bears its pale yellow-green flowers, not showy but blessed with a rich, airborne evening fragrance. These pretty shrubs both form neat mounds of evergreen foliage and deserve a place by the house door you use most often; but give them deep, moist soil and shelter from drying winds and sun.

Showier than these is *Viburnum* × *burkwoodii*, a semi-evergreen shrub about 1.8 m (6 ft) high with rounded clusters of carnation-scented white flowers opening from pink buds. It is easier to grow, and has a longer though less concentrated season of flower, than the familiar *V. carlesii*, which loses all its matt green leaves in winter. *V.* × *burkwoodii* could form the centrepiece of a spring group in your evening garden, with fragrant white narcissi such as 'Actaea', like a larger version of the wild white narcissus of alpine meadows. Sweet rocket (*Hesperis matronalis*) flowers in late spring; its rich perfume, redolent of cloves, carries furthest on the evening air. This metre-high herbaceous plant comes in white or lilac varieties – the white shows best at dusk – and seeds itself, so you can quickly build up a drift of it around your shrubs.

For summer you can add white roses. There is a wide choice: old-fashioned kinds like the once-flowering damask rose 'Madame Hardy'; a repeat-flowering shrub rose such as *R. rugosa* 'Blanc Double de Coubert'; or a modern rose specially bred for fragrance, perhaps the cluster-flowered 'Margaret Merrill', blush white and deliciously sweet. The Madonna lily, *Lilium candidum*, has flowers of crystalline white with rich golden stamens (Fig. 10). It is one of the easier lilies so long as you grow

Fig. 10 The Madonna lily, *Lilium candidum*, has crystalline white flowers with an exquisite fragrance.

no others, or restrain yourself to those you grow from seed, such as *Lilium regale*. In this way the Madonna lily should avoid infection by crippling viruses. And then there are white phloxes, which add their peppery aroma in high summer. 'Mia Ruys' is a good choice, at 45 cm (18 in) tall, for a small garden.

The modern, brightly coloured tobacco flowers, bred to stay open all day, have lost much of their scent. For your evening garden you must turn to the old *Nicotiana affinis*, which has white, green-backed flowers opening as the light fades, and all the fragrance you could wish for. Much taller than this is *N. sylvestris*, with big rosettes of pale green, sticky, weed-smothering foliage, and spires of long-tubed white trumpets. By day it is handsome; by night, deliciously scented as well.

PERFUMES OF THE NIGHT

It's not only white flowers that are valuable to the busy gardener. Some night-fragrant flowers are coloured, such as evening primroses, the biennial *Oenothera odorata* with wide yellow cups opening in the evening. *Mirabilis jalapa*, the marvel of Peru or four o'clock plant – so called for its habit of opening at teatime – has multi-coloured flowers of red and yellow, and sometimes also of cream, primrose, pink and white. It does have rather coarse foliage; but at night, inhaling its perfume, you won't see it.

Cestrum parqui, a tall half-shrubby plant, is related to the tobaccos and has foliage with the rather disagreeable smell common to the family. But its plumes of yellow-green flowers are handsome, and from late evening they are very fragrant. It is a hardy cousin of the queen of the night, renowned all over the world for its night perfume. Unlike some other plants you could include for evening scent, the cestrum has no daytime fragrance at all.

Petunias are tobacco relatives too, and some – especially the blue-flowered kinds – are fragrant at night. Of course, as half-hardy annuals they are a little more demanding to grow from seed, as are the tobaccos

Opposite: above left: One of the best evergreen shrubs to plant near a door, in a shady spot, is *Daphne pontica*, for its rich sweet night fragrance in spring. *Above right:* Several carnation-scented viburnums have white flowers in spring. *V. carlesii* 'Diana' opens from rich pink buds. *Below left:* The perfume of *Lilium speciosum* evokes tropical nights; just one bloom will fill a room with its rich scent. *Below right:* The exotic, perfumed *Datura suaveolens* can be grown outside in a large tub in summer, and brought in to shelter from the frost all winter.

themselves, than plants like sweet rocket which you can leave alone to perpetuate themselves. But even busy people may find a moment or two to pop a few seeds of each in a tray, in warmth, during spring. Prick out the seedlings into trays, harden them off, and plant them out as spring yields to summer and the risk of frosts is past. Give the petunias light soil and plenty of sun; the tobaccos a richer, moister soil.

Nothing could be simpler to sow than the night-scented stock, *Matthiola bicornis*. This little annual, which you can grow easily by just scattering a few seeds where you want it to flower, is almost invisible by day, a dingy little plant with small lilac-brown flowers that open only at night, when they emit a powerful sweet airborne fragrance. Try growing it among more showy flowers below a window that you are likely to open and sit by on summer evenings.

There is quite another class of colours, apart from white and very pale tones, that is of value at dusk. Though some shades of bright pink, carmine and purple can seem crude by day, for a short while at dusk they glow richly, with fire at their hearts. A billow of shocking pink phlox, or the blooms of the candy pink thornless Bourbon rose 'Zéphirine Drouhin' exemplify this quality and add too their quota of scent, the hot perfume of phloxes and the rich rose fragrance of 'Zéphirine'. *Verbena bonariensis*, a tall perennial relative of the low-growing bedding verbenas we've already met, has small heads of flower on branching, almost leafless stems: ideal for spearing through lower plants at the border's edge. Here it will be close to your nose and eye, for you to catch that moment when its violet-purple flowers seem to reflect the embers of the dying sun. Though a little tender, *V. bonariensis* sows itself happily, making it another good choice for the busy gardener.

You are unlikely to have drifts of *Lilium speciosum* the way you can have sweeps of these self-sowers. But this lily is so magnificent, and its flowers so powerfully fragrant, especially at night, that one or two bulbs are enough. It is variable in colour; some of the best kinds are those where the white of the flared, recurved petals is almost wholly overlaid by the crimson stain at its heart, giving this lily, too, the quality of luminosity at dusk. It is precious enough to grow in a pot, to keep on your patio or terrace, wherever you sit on warm evenings outside; or you could keep a plant indoors while in flower, for it will fill a house with its perfume and attract comment from every visitor.

If you have space to keep them frost-free in winter, the daturas, too, are grand plants best grown in tubs to decorate and perfume your sitting place on summer evenings. *Datura suaveolens*, a tender shrub, has long, hanging white trumpets with flared, curled-back lobes. These flowers are as powerfully scented as they are spectacular.

EASY-CARE FRAGRANCE

For many busy gardeners, the need is not only for plants they can enjoy
at dusk, but also plants for all day and all year, plants that are undemanding, attractive and, of course, fragrant. Hardy and easy shrubs, perennials
that don't need frequent lifting, splitting and replanting, bulbs that look
after themselves: these are what they want. We've already met the
honey-scented *Berberis sargentiana*, just the sort of good-tempered shrub
we need. For milder gardens at least, another easy-going evergreen is
Choisya ternata, the Mexican orange-blossom. Its glossy foliage is aromatic, with a pungency not everyone appreciates, but few will quarrel with
the fragrance of its white flowers in late spring, and often, again, in
summer.

Day lilies are the very type of perennial that needs little attention, and
can be left without division and resetting for several years. As we've
already seen, the yellow-flowered kinds are the ones with fragrance. One
that is especially good for commuters is *Hemerocallis citrina*, with narrow
lemon trumpets opening at teatime to emit their sweet perfume. Equally
undemanding are the hardy geraniums, but most are without scent.
Exceptionally, *G. macrorrhizum* has strongly aromatic leaves. Its flowers
come in magenta, pink or white, depending on the variety, and are borne
in early summer over mats of dense, weed-smothering foliage that often
turns to crimson in autumn.

Useful though such ground-covering plants can be, sometimes a spot
of weeding, on hands and knees, can give an unexpected bonus – as when
it brings you close to the sweet fragrance of grape hyacinths (*Muscari*).
This spring-flowering bulb, so familiar for its spikes of close-packed blue,
pinch-mouthed bells, is one of the easiest small bulbs to grow. Its foliage
is dense, lasting long enough to choke out many weeds. It will even cope
with the root competition at the base of a hedge, where it can be grown
in a thick band turning solidly blue with flower in spring.

For those with just a little more time to spare, some fragrant shrubs
that require annual or occasional pruning are easy to grow. Among them
we can include buddleias; the common butterfly bush needs no more
than a severe pruning in spring to remain shapely and stay within
bounds. Mock orange, varieties of *Philadelphus*, can be pruned immedi-
ately after flowering, when old, much-branched stems are removed to
keep the bush free of disfiguring dead wood. And, of course, there is the
great family of roses; but these will have a chapter to themselves.

CHAPTER 6

FRAGRANCE IN THE HOUSE

FRAGRANT FLOWERS AND LEAVES TO PICK

When you prune your mock orange, in the manner I suggested in the previous chapter, you could anticipate by a week or two the 'correct' time to prune by cutting branches while they are still in flower, and bringing them into the house. It is worth, then, taking a few moments to strip off the leaves: the flowers show better and last longer. Be warned, though: the flowers of mock orange are so powerfully scented, especially the old *Philadelphus coronarius* and its varieties, with creamy white flowers, that some people cannot cope with them indoors.

The trick of stripping leaves works – indeed, is all but essential – with many other flowering shrubs too. Crushing or splitting woody stem-ends, holding the cut ends in boiling water for a few moments, and soaking the cut branches in deep water overnight before arranging them in vases: these are all ways of making sprays of flowering shrubs last longer in water.

Almost any fragrant shrub that is large enough for you to cut from can yield blooms for the house. I was once lucky enough to be able to cut branches almost as tall as me from the willow-leaved magnolia, *M. salici-folia*, in bud. As they opened, the pure white flowers filled the room with their rich, orange-blossom perfume. Vases of lilac, bowls of old-fashioned roses: these are classics of fragrance. If you have access to a lime tree that you can lawfully cut from, try bringing the branches in flower indoors; stripped bare of their leaves, they are remarkably beautiful as well as fragrant.

While waiting for your shrubs to reach picking size – which won't be too many years in the case of the roses or of fast-growing shrubs such as

Opposite: above left: The wintersweet, *Chimonanthus praecox*, has a poignantly sweet fragrance and bears its waxy flowers all winter long. *Above right:* 'Manteau d'Hermine' is a dwarf variety of *Philadelphus* with double white flowers and a delicious orange-blossom fragrance. *Below left:* Lily of the valley is a favourite flower of spring for its sweet, fresh fragrance. *Below right: Hamamelis mollis* 'Pallida' is one of the best witch hazels, with a spicy sweet fragrance.

creamy, spring-flowering *Cytisus × praecox* – there are of course perennial and annual flowers to pick for indoors. I recall with nostalgia the
long hot summer I spent, many years ago, in an eighteenth-century
house in East Anglia which was opened to the public every Wednesday.
On Tuesdays we all spent several hours picking sweet peas from the long
rows, grown just for the purpose, in the walled kitchen garden. The
varieties were chosen, I am sure, for their fragrance rather than just their
colour, so there were few of the scarlet and salmon tones. Not everyone
is able to fill, as we did then, big silver bowls every week for a dozen
rooms, but as we've seen, sweet peas are not hard to grow. A short row
of them is within every gardener's capability.

Earlier in the year, in late spring, lily-of-the-valley (*Convallaria majalis*)
produces its exquisitely perfumed white bells. Now lily-of-the-valley is a
funny customer; it doesn't always appreciate your endeavours to give it
what all the books say it likes, a moist and humusy soil in part shade. But
let it once get a hold, and it is quite capable of running into a gravel path
or colonizing a patch of hard-baked clay, where it may well thrive.
Sooner or later the roots become congested and the flowers dwindle in
numbers. An easy way to remedy this is to cut out squares of root and
soil and fill the space with a good compost. The spadeful you have lifted
can be used to start a new colony elsewhere. It is worth growing both the
type and the slightly larger-flowered 'Fortin's Giant', which opens a fort-
night later, to give yourself the longest season of this charming flower.

Although day lilies, *Hemerocallis*, have short-lived individual flowers –
as their name implies, each one open only for a day – the stems normally
each bear several blooms. These will open in succession in water, making
day lilies as valuable to pick as they are in the border. By contrast, the
retiring little *Iris graminea* makes no floral contribution in the garden: its
small, purple flowers are hidden by dense clumps of narrow, strap-like
foliage. None the less, the plumtart iris has earned itself a place in many
gardeners' affections for its fragrance, which is indeed just like stewed
plums. It is a thoroughly good-tempered little plant which can be tucked
into an out-of-the-way, sunny corner to delight the nose in its early summer season.

Pinks and carnations (forms of *Dianthus*) come in many sizes, from
miniatures tiny enough for troughs and rock gardens to the long-
stemmed florists' carnation which, all too often, has no scent to speak of.
But many pinks and carnations have a rich clove perfume, and some have
intricately patterned petals – the so-called laced pinks – which gain from
the close inspection they receive in a vase, indoors. Both annual and perennial kinds can be had with this warm fragrance, and most have attractive glaucous foliage as well which is an asset in the border. Since

carnation seed germinates easily at low temperatures, and the plants need a long growing season to ensure a supply of flowers from high summer onwards, you can sow annual carnations in early autumn or in late winter. Overwinter autumn-sown plants in a cold frame; plant out, whether autumn or winter-sown, in mid-spring to let them make sturdy plants. Or, of course, you can grow them in pots to stand on your patio or by your front door. The Giant Chabaud and Enfant de Nice strains are excellent, while the newer Knight series are expensive, but come in separate colours as well as mixtures.

Stocks, which we have already discussed in Chapter 3, can also be cut and brought indoors. If you want them only for cutting, the column types are a good choice, forming a single spike instead of branching.

WINTER POSIES

Lovely though these summer flowers may be in the house, it is perhaps the fragrant shrubs of winter that give the most acute pleasure when picked and brought indoors. Most of the fragrant shrubs that flower in winter are fairly slow growing, so – at first, at least – the most that can be picked are sprays of this and sprigs of that, to form mixed, sweet-scented posies.

Foremost for fragrance among winter shrubs, as its name suggests, is the wintersweet, *Chimonanthus praecox*. It is not a handsome shrub, and takes several years to flower; it needs a good ripening to flower freely, such as would be provided if you give it a sunny wall to grow against. But when its translucent, starry flowers at last appear they exhale the most exquisite perfume. If you can acquire it, the waxy yellow-flowered 'Luteus' is the best, of clear tender colouring and all the sweetness of the type. A small branchlet, or even a few flowers tweaked off and floated in a bowl, will perfume a room.

Other shrubs of winter from which you could pick a little spray or two are the witch hazels. Not all of these are fragrant; to be certain of scent, you should buy your plant in flower. The common *Hamamelis mollis*, with warm yellow flowers, and 'Pallida', of paler lemon colouring showing up especially well against a dark background in the winter sun, both have the desired spicy fragrance; but few of the red-flowered kinds are scented. 'Feuerzauber' ('Magic Fire') in coppery red is one to look for. The later-flowering *H. japonica* 'Zuccariniana' has a coarser quality of scent. All bear their spidery flowers, composed of narrow, twisted, ribbon-like petals, on bare branches. The witch hazels prefer a neutral or acid soil, though given adequate moisture (not, however, a wet soil) they will grow on somewhat limy soils also.

By contrast, the winter-flowering viburnums will grow on any reasonable garden soil; they are hardy, and easy to grow. The fragrance of these deciduous winter-flowering viburnums carries far on the air when not blown away by blustery winter winds. Both *V. farreri* and its hybrid offspring *V.* × *bodnantense* smell strongly of almonds. The clusters of small white flowers, opening from pink buds, are borne on leafless branches over a long winter season. Beware: the evergreen laurustinus, *V. tinus*, is not fragrant.

The deciduous viburnums are not the only winter-flowering shrubs with a foody smell. The evergreen *Azara microphylla*, which needs a sheltered corner against a wall except in very mild gardens, bears minute yellow flowers on the undersides of its branches, concealed by the neat glossy foliage. But though insignificant, they smell exactly like custard powder, with the same vanilla scent.

Much smaller, and hardier, the sarcococcas are also evergreen shrubs flowering in winter. Their little flowers, composed of bunches of spiky, pinky white petals, are scarcely more showy than the azara's, but are welcome for their far-carrying honey aroma. In a vase, indoors, the daintiness of the little sprays of flower can be appreciated, and the neat foliage – almost reminiscent of a small bamboo – is a pretty foil for other flowers. In the garden, sarcococcas are better in light shade than in full sun, where the narrow green leaves can turn to a sickly yellow.

The winter-flowering honeysuckles are not climbers, as are many of their summer counterparts, but they have just as sweet a scent. The creamy white flowers are small – look for *Lonicera* × *purpusii* for the largest, all of 2 cm ($\frac{3}{4}$ in) across – and borne on bare branches on a rather ungainly shrub, faster-growing than the witch hazels and viburnums. They are undemanding shrubs, and can well be tucked away where their plain summer appearance is unobtrusive.

One of the most charming and elegant winter flowers to pick and enjoy indoors is not borne on a shrub. *Iris unguicularis* used to be called *I. stylosa*, and is still often so labelled. To flower freely, this north African iris needs the sunniest position you can give it. Pick the flowers when they are still in scrolled bud – almost invisible, for the outside of the petals is buff-coloured. They will open rapidly in water in a warm room, to reveal their exquisite lavender colouring and delicate fragrance. They are lovely enough to deserve a vase to themselves.

FRAGRANT POTFULS

A much humbler flower is the snowdrop (*Galanthus*). Some named kinds have more of that honey fragrance than others; all reveal it only if you

The winter-flowering *Irish unguicularis*, better known as *I. stylosa*, opens from scrolled, buff-coloured buds to these exquisite, fragrant blooms.

approach close. You can lift a few bulbs as they first spear through, scooping up a trowelful of bulbs and soil together. Pack them into a pot of compost so you can enjoy them indoors. You can do the same with primroses and violets; though violets, with their habit of throwing out runner-like shoots, are harder to lift as a tidy clump. The little *Crocus chrysanthus* varieties, too, can be treated in this way. Keep all these hardy flowers in a cool room, and plant them outside again as soon as they have finished flowering, so they can build up strength again for next year.

There are, of course, the classic bulbs, specially treated, that you can buy to have in flower in winter indoors: hyacinths, narcissi. The original, wild *Cyclamen persicum* is also sweetly scented. Although the varieties bred for bigger, brighter flowers have lost their fragrance in the process, breeders have lately become aware of this quality once more. A new range of small-flowered kinds has been developed, many of which have some at least of the fragrance of the original and something, too, of its prettily marbled leaves. The petals of these kinds are broader than the narrow, elegantly twisted segments of the wildling, giving the flower a plumper look. The colour range is wider than the original pale pink or white, but the bright scarlet kinds are scentless still.

· CHAPTER 7 ·

TOUCH AND SMELL

More than any other art-form, a garden brings into play all our senses. Of course, the first impact is visual; and the object of this book is to bring an increased awareness of the sense of smell in the garden. Then again, part of the tranquillity of a garden can be attributed to our sense of hearing: not through silence, but from the innumerable tiny sounds that build up into a feeling of peace. The falling patter of birch leaves, or the clatter of the larger, harder leaves of laurel in the wind; raindrops hissing on to warm soil; running water; bird song; the hum of bees in a patch of winter heather or on a quilt of pink sedum in late summer; all these combine with the sounds of human activity outside the garden precincts to emphasize the sense of an oasis of our own creation.

The sense of taste is one in which all those who grow vegetables and herbs can indulge, but beyond these there remains a fifth: the sense of touch. This, I believe, is curiously neglected by many gardeners, especially those beguiled by the visual impact of our brightest flowers. And yet it seems an instinctive reaction to run your hand up a spike of lavender in flower, so as to release its tangy sweet perfume – as anyone whose garden is open to the public at lavender time will find to their cost, when at the end of the day the proud purple spikes are reduced to a forest of bare stems. And everyone who recognizes the plant will pluck and crush a leaf of lemon verbena (*Aloysia triphylla*) to inhale its tart fragrance.

AROMATIC PLANTS TO BRUSH AGAINST

OR CRUSH

Many are the aromatic plants that give most freely of their fragrance when stroked, rubbed or brushed against. If you plant them by a path's edge, or around a patio, you will find another bonus of touch and of scent from your garden.

Most aromatics need full sun to concentrate the essential oils that give them their characteristic perfume. Full sun also suits silver and grey plants, several of which are as aromatic, and as welcoming to the touch, as lavender. There are, indeed, several different lavenders to choose from. Many people select, on visual grounds, one of the dwarfer kinds such as purple-spiked 'Hidcote', but the leaves of this variety are narrow and less silvery than those of the old English lavender. This, a larger bush, has paler spikes on a well-filled bush, with the best perfume. The French lavender, *L. stoechas*, has cockaded purple flowers and a slightly different aroma.

Botanists often recognize, in the names they give to plants, a likeness to another plant. So with *Salvia lavandulifolia*, a sage but with narrow grey leaves slightly reminiscent of lavender, and a rather different aroma from the typical sage, less foody and more akin to perfumery. It makes a very pleasing low, mounded shrub, good cover against weeds on a sunny bank. The name may not be authentic, but it is the one nurserymen use. With the sage and the lavenders, on your sunny slope or by a hot patio wall, try other greys such as *Caryopteris* × *clandonensis* and the Russian sage, *Perovskia atriplicifolia*. Both have blue flowers in late summer and pungently aromatic foliage, the first sweeter than the distinctly turpentine aroma of the second. Both have named kinds that are worth seeking out: 'Kew Blue' and 'Heavenly Blue' are good *Caryopteris* varieties, and 'Blue Spire' with neatly dissected leaves is the best Russian sage. Don't try eating it; it is not a sage, nor indeed Russian!

Another misleading name belongs to *Santolina*, called cotton lavender though it is not a lavender. Most have silvery foliage, tight-packed in the common *S. incana* and feathery in *S. neapolitana*. This last is more pleasing also in flower, with pale lemon button flowers in place of the more familiar plant's vivid yellow.

Like all these grey and silver plants, the silvery artemisias need stroking. 'Powis Castle' and 'Lambrook Silver' are both so silky soft that this is a real pleasure, while the quieter grey-green *A. abrotanum* or lad's love is feathery soft also, an old cottage favourite for a warm spot by a path where it can be caressed in passing for its sharp fresh scent.

FRAGRANCE AT YOUR FEET

Also sun-loving are the thymes, much lower-growing plants that you are more likely to scuff with your toe than stoop to stroke. With their carpeting habit they adapt well to growing among paving stones, rooting in the cracks and spreading out over the surface. They will not take constant traffic, however, so you should plant them to the edges of your path or patio. Varieties of *Thymus serpyllum* are the most suitable, forming a ground-hugging mat of green or grey foliage, spangled in summer with tiny flowers, white, pink, crimson or purple. They all smell fairly

Many aromatic plants need to be lightly bruised to release their essential oils. Here, thyme and lavender mingle with foliage plants and spill onto paving.

similar, but *T. herba-barona*, which looks much like a *serpyllum* variety, smells exactly like caraway seed when bruised.

The low-growing form of chamomile, *Anthemis nobilis* 'Treneague', is often recommended for lawns, for it forms interlacing mats of stems decked with fresh green foliage that, when disturbed, emits a powerful aroma of apples. However, as with the thymes, it is not wholly weed-proof, and whereas with a grass lawn you can use selective weedkillers to kill everything but the grass, there is no equivalent for chamomile or thyme. Grown in the cracks in paving, or in the space where a single slab has been removed, this question of weeds will be less of a problem than if you attempt an entire lawn.

It may be that your patio has a shaded corner, where thymes and

Left: The Warminster broom, *Cytisus × praecox*, has a heavy perfume too strong for some, but a spray in a vase adds fragrance to a mixed bouquet.

Right: **Fig. 11** *Monarda didyma* is called bergamot or Oswego tea, for its aromatic leaves can be brewed.

chamomile would not thrive. For such a spot one of the little creeping mints would be a good choice. The larger is pennyroyal, *Mentha pulegium*, with neat darkish foliage and spikes, ankle-high or taller, of purple-mauve flowers. A fraction its size, but much more powerfully pungent, is *Mentha requienii*, a mere film of minute fresh green foliage spreading over soil or moist stones and bearing flowers so small you almost need a hand-lens to see them.

A much larger herbaceous plant that is worth planting where you can stroke its aromatic foliage is bergamot, *Monarda didyma* (Fig. 11). This, too, prefers a moist rather than dry soil, but needs some sun. The basal foliage forms a mat that needs fairly frequent replanting to keep it in good order, but this is no hardship when every movement of the trowel frees its perfume, like a concentrated whiff of Earl Grey tea. The claw-shaped flowers, borne in summer, are set in whorls, two or three tiers of them, up the stems. 'Cambridge Scarlet' is more crimson than scarlet, and there are pink, purple and magenta kinds also.

For sunnier spots with sharper drainage there is catmint, varieties of *Nepeta*, which are often teamed with roses. The grey foliage and spikes of blue-mauve flowers of *Nepeta × faassenii* and others like it assort with roses of virtually any colour, or could join the other aromatic greys already suggested for a hot and sunny bank. Although this is not the genuine catmint, all nepetas are tempting to cats, and you may need to insinuate some thorny branches of berberis or gorse among the catmint stems to prevent the clump being flattened by intoxicated cats.

FRAGRANT HERBS AS ORNAMENTALS

Nepeta is sometimes included in herb gardens, though it has no culinary use. If you have space, and the time to devote to keeping it tidy and under control, a herb garden can be a most decorative as well as a fragrant and aromatic place full of delights for the cook. But though the idea of herbs in between the spokes of a cartwheel laid flat, or the rungs of a ladder, or in beds edged with clipped box or santolina or germander (*Teucrium*), is very appealing, such conceits are a good deal of work. Another approach is to treat the prettier herbs as ornamentals, and relegate the ones that are merely flavourful without being beautiful to a corner of the vegetable patch.

Take, for example, the purple-leaved sage, *Salvia officinalis* 'Purpurascens'. This is just as tasty as the plain grey-green kind, and its soft greyed purple makes a gentle companion for flowers of pink or purple colouring, or for pale yellow. Try it, for example, with *Cytisus* × *praecox*, a medium-sized broom enjoying the same good drainage and sunny conditions as the sage, and adding not only a mass of creamy primrose flower in spring, but also its own characteristic strong fragrance. The purple form of basil, well-named 'Black Opal', is a handsome half-hardy herb with a splendid Mediterranean aroma; you could team it with yellow flowers or add it to a border of reds and purples for a bold effect in summer.

Most of the mints prefer some moisture, and the white-variegated form of apple mint, *Mentha rotundifolia* 'Variegata', must have shade too, for its pale foliage burns in full sun. It has a slightly different perfume from the plain green apple mint; whenever you weed among your shrubs where you have allowed this mint to spread, or simply when you go into the border to pick a spray of this or that, you will release its fragrance. Another lowly, spreading plant for similar conditions is *Houttuynia cordata*. The type plant has dark green, bronzed heart-shaped foliage and white flowers, which are more showy in the double-flowered variety. Recently a jazzy variegated form has been introduced, the leaves marked with magenta, pink and cream. Grown in full sun this will be most brightly coloured and less apt to spread enthusiastically. All have the same pungent aroma when bruised, like the smell of orange peel with a throat-catching hint of something less agreeable.

CHAPTER 8

THE QUEEN OF FLOWERS

The rose holds such a special place in all our hearts, and roses are such a varied lot, that they deserve a chapter of their own. I do not propose to make great lists of fragrant roses: that would need a whole book, of which there are already many for interested gardeners to turn to. Instead, I will pick out representatives of the main types of scented rose, with some ideas on how to grow them.

For several reasons, I believe it is often better to grow your roses in company with other plants rather than in conventional rose beds. Roses are prone to disease — some more than others, it's true — and the more they are packed together with other roses, the more easily such diseases can spread. And then, by mixing your roses with other plants, you make opportunities to create beautiful pictures, while the roses will bring fragrance to many groups that might otherwise lack this extra dimension.

THE OLD ROSES

Devotees of the old-fashioned roses often maintain that their perfume cannot be matched by modern kinds. But beware, not all old roses are fragrant. Those that are — and they are many — are found in all the major groups of old roses, with such evocative names as the damask rose, the roses of Provins or gallicas, the Provence or cabbage roses, the albas, the Bourbon and the moss roses. Let us consider this last group first, for some people seem to believe that any old-fashioned rose is a moss rose. Not so. Moss roses are so-called because of the sticky, fragrant, moss-like glands covering the stalk and sepals (the green outer guard to the coloured petals). This 'moss' may be green or dark and bronzed: a white rose with dark moss, such as 'Blanche Moreau', has particular charm. The flowers of moss roses are of the typical flat-faced, full-petalled old-rose style; most are wonderfully fragrant, perhaps none more than the common pink moss itself. But other colours can be had apart from pink and white. Try 'Nuits de Young', with deepest black-crimson flowers and dark foliage, among the pale yellow perennial foxglove *Digitalis grandiflora*, and a background of fresh pale green foliage. Or, space permitting, you could grow the tall grey-lilac flowered 'William Lobb' among silvery foliage.

Fig. 12 Rose 'Celestial' has scented, shell-pink flowers. Its blue-grey foliage is echoed by the cream and grey-blue leaves of *Iris pallida* 'Aureo Variegata'.

Many moss roses originated as 'sports' of the Provence, centifolia or cabbage rose. These are all names for the full-petalled, gracefully swan-necked roses, full of far-carrying perfume, beloved of many painters of flowers from the Dutch old masters to Fantin-Latour and later artists. One of these roses, indeed, is named after Fantin-Latour: a vigorous and handsome rose of clear pale pink, full of petals and of scent. Like the moss roses, the centifolias come in pink, creamy or blush white, cerise, and near-violet. They flower in summer only. You could set the clear pink *Rosa centifolia* itself, the original of the group, among the tall blue-cupped *Campanula persicifolia* 'Telham Beauty'. Its crested variety, *R. centifolia cristata* or 'Chapeau de Napoleon', is so called because the calyx is winged and crested to resemble a three-cornered hat. The flowers are otherwise similar. If the deeper violet-crimson tones appeal, choose 'Tour de Malakoff'; for tiny spaces, select the miniature pink 'De Meaux'.

The alba rose 'Celeste' (or 'Celestial') has a flower of considerable charm and elegance, not as sumptuous as the Provence roses, but opening from pointed, scrolled buds to a semi-double flower of pure pale pink set among greyish foliage (Fig. 12). A rose of such subtlety deserves the best

The Bourbon rose 'Madame Isaac Pereire' is generous in every way, with perhaps the most intense fragrance of any rose.

of companions: *Iris pallida dalmatica* for its strong, glaucous, sword-shaped leaves echoing the grey-tinted rose foliage. The pungent-smelling, metallic blue ferny foliage of rue would add another note of form and aroma alike. The 'Queen of Denmark' is another famous alba, with full flowers of richer pink. In this group, too, is found the White Rose of York, but this and 'Great Maiden's Blush', another well-loved old kind, are large shrubs too expansive for most modern gardens.

Also in the alba group is the York and Lancaster rose, so called because the flowers are part white, part pink. It is not, however, truly a striped rose. Striped blooms occur among several groups of old roses, notably the gallicas. This is a group of compact, almost thornless bushes holding their flowers upright, not nodding like the centifolia types. The colours of the gallicas tend to the deeper shades, mauve, purple and maroon, with mid pink and a few paler shades, and several striped kinds. The brightest of these is the oldest, 'Rosa Mundi' or 'Versicolor', striped in pale and deep pink. It sometimes reverts to its parent, the bright crimson-pink 'Officinalis'. Both make a fine floral hedge, or can join other shrubs in a mixed group. If you are going to make a hedge of them, prepare the ground well, digging in humus and fertilizer, then set the plants 1m (3ft) apart. They can be lightly clipped with shears in early spring to keep them compact. Such a hedge would be a pretty and practical division between the ornamental and the vegetable garden, delightfully scented in their single, but extended, summer season.

Of more formal flower shape is 'Camaieux', another striped bloom of softer colouring, cream, lilac and grey-pink. It assorts well with 'Belle de Crécy', of similar colouring but unstriped.

Almost as evocative as the words 'moss rose' is the name 'damask rose'. This somewhat varied group is chiefly characterized by soft, greyish foliage and pale blooms in white or blush to clear pink. Some of the white kinds, such as 'Leda', are stained with crimson at the edge of the petals. As with all the other groups there are many that could claim our attention, but perhaps the honour should go to 'Madame Hardy'. This beautifully formal, flat-faced, quartered creamy white bloom displays a green button-eye which only adds to its charm. Although, in common with most old roses, 'Madame Hardy' flowers once only, she would make an exquisite centrepiece to a grouping of white flowers for evening effect.

With the Bourbon roses we come to a group that habitually flowers in summer and again in autumn. Indeed, the autumn floraison is often superior to the first flush. The Bourbons retain the 'old-fashioned' shape of flower, but display also the silky petals of the China roses, distant ancestors of our modern roses. Because of these qualities, allied to a delicious fragrance, it is harder than ever to choose just one or two representatives of the Bourbon roses. For fragrance, the palm should go to 'Madame Isaac Pereire', possibly the most intensely fragrant of all roses. The big flowers are an assertive shade of magenta-rose and full of petals. So generous a rose needs rich living to give of its best, and bold companions to match its vigour. *Hosta sieboldiana* 'Elegans', with broad, ribbed, glaucous-blue leaves, is of a size to appear in scale. Another Bourbon rose, lilac-pink 'Louise Odier', has already received mention in Chapter 2.

FRAGRANT SHRUB ROSES

There are plenty of fragrant blooms to be found among the many shrub roses that do not fall into these old-rose categories. Some are wild roses, or their near derivatives; other are more highly bred, yet still shrub-like, less formal than the modern large-flowered hybrid tea roses. Some groups of roses are especially valuable for fragrance: the scotch roses, the rugosas and the hybrid musks in particular. The scotch or burnet roses, *R.*

spinosissima and its varieties, grow wild in Britain as well as further north and east, from Iceland to Siberia and south to Armenia. They are thus extremely frost-hardy. They have in common their suckering habit and their ferociously prickly and bristly stems, very neat ferny foliage, and small flowers borne in early summer. Their perfume is potent, sweet and fresh. Furthermore, they are tough and willing to grow, and to flower abundantly, in even the poorest of soils. For all these qualities they were once immensely popular, and many varieties were raised. Now, few are available: a double white and a double blush, both with little globular blooms, are those you are most likely to encounter. A rose to treasure is 'Stanwell Perpetual', a sweetly fragrant pale pink hybrid of the scotch rose which, as its name implies, flowers on after its main, midsummer burst.

With their ability to grow in dry, sandy soils, these burnet roses can well join pink and white cistus, and bushes of rosemary and lavender, in a grouping of fragrant and aromatic shrubs in full sun. But they do just as well on clay, as in the garden where I grew up. Here, in an awkwardly shaped corner where a lawn, a box hedge and a paved path meet, the double white *R. spinosissima* forms a solid, weed-excluding clump about 1 m (3 ft) high, smothered in bloom in early summer year after year, with no more attention than a quick clip-over with shears whenever it grows forward over the path.

Of quite a different style are the rugosa roses, though these too have the ability to grow on almost any soil, especially impoverished sand; and like the scotch roses they too tend to sucker when grown on their own roots. But they are bolder in their ribbed, rich green foliage, which in autumn turns corn-gold where the ferny leaflets of the burnet roses takes on quieter bronze and plum tones. In flower they are much larger too, with elegant scrolled buds opening to wide single or loose double flowers from late spring to autumn. The typical colour is vivid magenta, but pale pink and pure white also occur. Their perfume is rich, spicy, and free on the air. The double-flowered kinds produce no fruit, but the single flowers of the type and its white form, and of pale pink 'Frau Dagmar Hastrup', are followed by big tomato-red hips borne among the later blooms. The finest doubles are magenta 'Roseraie de l'Hay' and white 'Blanc Double de Coubert'. As a flowering and fragrant hedge the rugosas are even finer than *R. gallica* 'Officinalis' and 'Versicolor'. As specimen shrubs, or components of the mixed border, they are equally valuable. The petals can be used to add extra fragrance to a cup of Earl Grey tea, and from the hips a conserve rich in vitamin C can be made.

The hybrid musk roses are a more varied group than the rugosas, but all make good large shrubs, most with extremely fragrant flowers. These are borne in high summer, as the old roses are fading, and continue until their abundant autumn climax. Their fragrance has that precious quality of floating free on the air for yards around. Two of them have already received mention in an earlier chapter: 'Moonlight' with creamy white flowers and mahogany-plum young growths, and the apricot-cream 'Buff Beauty'. Others can be had in pink – coral 'Cornelia', silvery 'Felicia' or blush 'Penelope' among them, the first and last in particular with a rich, musky perfume. 'Penelope' is one of the finest, with bright coral buds opening to loose creamy pink flowers which fade to near-white in hot weather. They are beautiful with gentle tones of pale blue flowers and grey foliage, or set among the sharp lime-yellow froth of *Alchemilla mollis*. Later 'Penelope', like other hybrid musks, produces huge sprays of autumn flower, and finally – unlike most – rounded, soft coral-pink hips.

There are so many fragrant roses that, even taking them group by group in this way, and relegating the climbing roses to Chapter 4, they risk taking more than their share of this book. So I can do no more, to conclude this chapter, than glance quickly at a few roses which have particular characteristics of fragrance.

In a few cases the aroma of rose foliage is as valuable as floral perfume. The incense rose, *R. primula*, is so called because of the fragrance of its young growths; the single yellow flowers are borne in late spring. The leaves of the sweet briar, *R. rubiginosa*, on the other hand, emit an aroma of apples, especially when carried on a warm, moist breeze. Another very beautiful wild rose with fragrance of both flower and leaf is *R. multibracteata*. This big shrub has greyish foliage and many small, lilac-pink flowers in high summer. Its gorgeous, very vigorous hybrid 'Cerise Bouquet' has similar foliage but much larger, double, vivid cerise flowers with a powerful rich, fruity perfume.

'Cerise Bouquet' is just one of many newer shrub roses – roses, that is, of the present century. They come in many sizes, styles and colours, and some are wonderfully fragrant. 'Aloha', which lends itself to growing as a pillar rose, is one such, already mentioned in Chapter 4. Then there is 'Constance Spry', a fitting tribute to a flower arranger who greatly loved, and helped to popularize, the old roses. A big shrub, it bears clear pink wide double flowers on arching stems. The fragrance is unusual, with overtones of myrrh.

A small group of modern shrub roses with names prefixed 'Frühlings', because of their late spring flowering season, derives from the Scotch roses. Though much larger in leaf, flower and growth than *R. spinosissima*, they too are extremely fragrant. 'Frühlingsgold' is a single yellow with a rich, spicy and fruity fragrance carrying for yards. Superficially similar in flower, but blooming later and lasting longer, is 'Golden

Fragrant roses mingle with lavender and the tall white *Galtonia candicans* to bring colour and scent to a patio.

Wings'. Try these yellow roses with a carpet of *Geranium* 'Johnson's Blue' at their feet, with contrasting sword-shaped foliage of irises or day lilies.

Modern roses of the hybrid tea and floribunda types come and go, succumbing far sooner than the shrub or old roses to the debility brought on by too much intensive propagation. Think of the once-popular sweet-scented roses that are now crippled by mildew, or simply unobtainable from suppliers; these may be exemplified by 'Fragrant Cloud'. It is harder, therefore, to recommend roses of this type for their fragrance, although plenty exist and more are introduced each year. Survivors from before the wars, such as shell-pink 'Ophelia' or the slightly deeper 'Madame Butterfly', still valued for their beautiful, elegant blooms and delicious fragrance, are the exceptions. The well-loved floribunda 'Iceberg', which if given its head will make a fair-sized shrub, seems to retain its good constitution. Let us hope that the much newer, smaller-growing blush-white 'Margaret Merrill', one of the most fragrant of modern roses, will prove as long-lived.

The shrub roses classed by their raiser as English roses, new roses in the old tradition, show signs of remaining with us thanks to their good constitution. Mr David Austin has introduced many of these bushy, chiefly very fragrant roses using the blood of old roses to give them the characteristic flower-shape, cupped or quartered, mixed with newer kinds from which they derive their recurrent-flowering qualities, and a wider range of colours than the truly old roses.

Some are short-growing, no larger than the average Hybrid Tea though more bushy and relaxed in appearance. The Chaucer series were the first to be named, and indeed one of the best is named 'Chaucer' after the great English poet. The cupped, rose-pink flowers are strongly fragrant of myrrh. 'The Reeve', of dusky deep pink with more globular flowers, has a fragrance more akin to the old roses, while the 'Wife of Bath' is a pet for small gardens, of neat growth with cupped, rose-pink flowers, myrrh-scented, produced constantly on a bush of tough constitution.

Another series is called after Shakespearean characters: dramatic dusky purple-crimson 'Othello', with a rich old-rose fragrance, and taller 'Cymbeline', with unusual grey-pink colouring and myrrh fragrance, among them.

Also in the Shakespeare series are several roses with colouring not found among the old roses. 'Perdita', bearing quartered flowers of apricot-blush colouring, won the Henry Edland Medal for fragrance from the Royal National Rose Society in 1984. Taller and deeper apricot in colour is 'Leander', with a sharp fruity fragrance; its companion 'Hero' is of unusually pure pink colouring with a rich fragrance.

Pure yellow is found in the most popular of all these roses, named 'Graham Thomas' in honour of the man who, more than any other single person, helped to popularise the old roses. The cupped, richly coloured flowers have a strong Tea Rose fragrance and appear in unbroken succession. 'Yellow Charles Austin', of clear lemon yellow, is a sport from the taller-growing 'Charles Austin', which bears large, cupped flowers of apricot yellow. Both the original and its pure yellow sport have a powerful fruity fragrance.

Because they flower repeatedly, these English roses need the same generous treatment as you would accord to your Hybrid Teas. They are pruned differently, however. As always when pruning, any dead, damaged or diseased growths should be removed. This done, some of the oldest growths may be removed, when they can be spared, to allow young shoots to spring from the base. The remaining branches may be cut back to about half their length.

CHAPTER 9

BRINGING THEM UP TO THE NOSE

Fragrance is not confined to plants that are tall enough for us to reach them without stooping. To enjoy the perfume of little plants without grovelling on hands and knees, we may need to resort to various ruses. The principle is simple: if we are not prepared to go down to tiny plants, they must come up to us – in raised beds, troughs, containers, walls, windowboxes . . .

BUILDING A WALL OF FRAGRANCE

Provided you are reasonably able-bodied, one of the most satisfying forms of what the trade calls 'hard landscaping' – building things, rather than planting them – is the construction of a drystone wall. Your wall can either be set against a bank, to retain the soil, or form the sides of a raised bed. You need, of course, a supply of suitable stones. Flattish pieces are easier to use than irregularly-shaped stones, but even with these a good-looking and solid wall can be built, with care. The bottom course of stones should be set into the soil and slightly tilted, so that the wall will be gradually stepped into the bank, or inwards to the centre of your raised bed. This 'batter', as it is called, is essential for stability.

As your wall goes up, each course of stones should be settled with some fine soil in place of the mortar you would use for a conventional wall. At the same time, the soil behind the wall should be well rammed in. It is most important to avoid air spaces behind the stones. First, they make for weakness. Second, as your wall goes up so you can tuck in plants; this is much easier than trying to tease the roots between the stones after the wall is built. But if, once establishing itself, the growing roots of your little fragrant pink or wallflower find no soil, only empty space, they will shrivel and your plant will die.

The base of a drystone wall is often a good place for plants that need extra ripening, such as *Iris unguicularis*, the winter-flowering iris described in Chapter 6. Plant it, not between the stones, but in the soil hard up against them. Where the wall faces away from full exposure to the sun, which this iris demands, the soil is likely to remain moist. Here you could tuck in a few primroses for their delicate fragrance in early spring.

As the wall goes up, so the opportunities for fragrant plants increase as they come nearer the nose. For sunny positions, clove-scented pinks (*Dianthus*) are ideal, enjoying the warmth of the stones. Their glaucous foliage is a pretty foil for flowers of white, pink or plum, often with a contrasting dark eye or laced with edging and markings of varying shades. There are many different named kinds to choose from, growing to 8–10 cm (3–4 ins), or you could raise a mixed batch from seed, selecting the prettiest and the sweetest for your wall.

In such a wall, wallflowers will often take on their true character as perennials, forming bushy plants on which the flowers, of many different colours, are borne in spring. Wallflowers too have a warm perfume with hints of clove. Closely related to the common bedding wallflower is a compact little, pale yellow *Erysimum* called 'Moonlight', with a fragrance nearer cinnamon than clove. Paler still is *E. capitatum*, with palest creamy primrose flowers and a strong, sweet perfume.

For the top of your wall, or in your raised bed, dwarf forms of santolina or of the curry plant, *Helichrysum*, will make neat silvery mounds each with a distinctive aroma. Alpine-growers would no doubt disapprove, but if you are seeking fragrance above all you could well plant some low-growing annuals among them. Several have received mention in Chapter 3. Others you could try include lilac-and-white *Ionopsidium acaule*, which is honey-scented; or fringe-petalled, white *Schizopetalum walkeri*, which smells sweetest at night.

It may be that a more formal wall will better meet your needs: mortared brick, or even concrete blocks can be used, though these last can look very stark if not well concealed with plenty of trailing plants masking the hard edges. If you can obtain them, old railway sleepers make an attractive low 'wall' to retain soil; but gone are the days when sleepers could be picked up for a few pence.

TROUGHS AND SINKS

Alpine enthusiasts like to grow their little plants in troughs. Again, genuine old stone troughs are now increasingly hard to obtain. This has given rise to a keen trade in old glazed sinks, now themselves almost as elusive. If you can find some, they can be disguised with a mixture known as hypertufa, which is a blend of cement, sand and peat mixed to a stiff porridge and applied to the sink. First make sure your sink is absolutely clean; then apply a coating of Unibond or Polybond glue and allow it to dry to tackiness. Slap on the hypertufa, using gloved hands to pat it to an even – but not *too* even – surface. Do be sure to do this after you have settled your sink where you want it to remain! Once the hypertufa is dry, crock the sink well and fill it with a suitable compost: a good John Innes No. 3 will do if you are intending to grow undemanding annuals or pinks.

Whatever method you use to bring small, fragrant plants nearer to the nose, such raised beds have particular value for the disabled, who can bring a wheelchair close up against the plants. At greater expense, special beds can be created which are table-shaped; that is, where there is provision for the wheelchair to slide under the projecting edge of the bed, so that a disabled gardener can not only smell the plants, but also work among them from a chair.

SCENTED GARDENS FOR THE BLIND

Blind people rely especially on the sense of smell and of touch in the garden. For them, plants to stroke, and plants with freely airborne fragrance, are precious. Particular care must of course be taken to ensure that there are no spiky plants to give an unwelcome surprise, so roses should be chosen with care. Those grown to the back of a bed are likely to be more appreciated than those which may hook the unwary, unseeing hand with a ferocious thorn.

The blind are more likely than many of us to appreciate the different aromas of tree foliage: the fruity thuyas are quite distinct from the parsley-like Lawson's cypress, *Chamaecyparis lawsoniana*, however similar they may appear in foliage to the sighted. Several firs have citrus tones in the aroma of their foliage, while the balsam fir, *Abies balsamea*, is so-called because of its scent. Among broad-leaved trees, one in particular has an unmistakable smell for a brief season, as the falling leaves lie on the ground. Many people liken it to strawberry jam. To me, it is hot toffee; if jam, then definitely overcooked, burnt jam. This extraordinary, far-carrying aroma belongs to *Cercidiphyllum japonicum*, a tree of great charm not only for this characteristic but also for its looks. Young leaves of the rounded shape, similar to the Judas tree or *Cercis*, which give it its botanical name, emerge shrimp pink; in autumn they turn gold.

Some plants can confuse by similarities, visual or aromatic, with other quite different species. Take *Hebe cupressoides*, a rounded shrub around 1 m (3 ft) high which has a dwarf form, 'Boughton Dome', well suited to one of the raised beds suggested earlier in this chapter. This evergreen shrub has greyish-blue foliage of a very conifer-like aspect, and when stroked smells exactly like a pencil cedar, yet it is related to the veronicas. I suspect, though, that most blind people, with their much more acute sense of smell than normal, would not be taken in by this, any more than they would think that *Philadelphus* 'Beauclerk' was a fresh pineapple.

CHAPTER 10

THE SCENTED CONSERVATORY

There is now such a wide range of conservatories available, from grand custom-made constructions for period houses to simple structures hardly more elaborate than a greenhouse, that almost anyone can afford one. Even space, or lack of it, need hardly be an obstacle: several London houses with tiny gardens have their conservatory on the roof instead of on the ground. And even a porch, if not too dark, can double as a tiny conservatory with one or two fragrant plants to delight the nose as you return home.

A conservatory, from which frost is excluded, enables us to grow some of the plants from warmer climates which have the rich, heavy perfume so typical of sub-tropical plants: gardenias, the tender jasmines, stephanotis. A well-grown gardenia, such as one sees on every plant stall in Italy, is a pleasure to behold with its glossy dark foliage, besides possessing one of the most delectable fragrances imaginable. Like the jasmines from warm climates – *J. polyanthum* is the best-known, and widely available – the flowers of gardenia are creamy white. Stephanotis needs warmer conditions and is consequently trickier to keep, but its waxy white flowers are richly scented. Like the jasmines, it is a twining plant. Another is *Hoya carnosa*, which will do with less heat than the stephanotis; the pink-flushed flowers have the aroma of incense, and hang their heads. You must be sure to train the stems with the leaves facing towards you, so that the flowers do the same. *Hoya bella* is less of a climber, and has blush flowers. The flowers of an unusual climber called *Wattakaka sinensis* are similar to those of hoya, white with a zone of red spots at their hearts, and a sweet perfume.

Another group of plants suitable for a frost-free conservatory are the lily-flowered rhododendrons such as 'Fragrantissimum'. Not only the shape, but also the perfume of the white flowers are like the lily. The oriental lily itself, *Lilium speciosum*, has a heavy perfume recalling that of the more powerfully scented jasmines. It can now be bought in flower at almost any season, in many shops and chain stores; or you can grow your own year after year by keeping the bulbs potted, but on the dry side (not dust-dry however) during winter. Then they will flower in summer – usually in the latter half of that season.

Fig. 13 *Gladiolus callianthus,* formerly known as *Acidanthera bicolor,* flowers in autumn.

FRAGRANT PLANTS IN POTS

Indeed, all these plants will grow in containers if you have not the sort of conservatory with beds of soil. Although plants in pots need particular attention to watering and feeding, and must be repotted at intervals, there are many advantages to containers over plants in beds. For one thing, you can shuffle them around so that the plants in flower are at the front, those temporarily looking a disgrace hidden at the back. Dormant plants can be tucked under the staging. This would be the place to keep your lilies, and also where hedychiums would spend the winter. The hedychiums are nearly-hardy members of the ginger family, with spires of spidery flowers in white, apricot or yellow, over bold broad foliage. *Hedychium gardnerianum* is one of the most handsome (and is commercially available), in yellow with protruding orange stamens. Its sideways-spreading roots need a big pot, and can be split in spring and repotted to make a small colony. The flowering season is late summer.

Several other plants with bulbous or cormous roots are worth space in a conservatory. Early in the year come the creamy white or pale yellow flowers of *Freesia refracta*, with a sweeter perfume than the coloured hybrids, pretty though these are. A much richer perfume comes from the flowers of *Eucharis grandiflora*, and most powerful of all is that of the tuberose, *Polianthes tuberosa*, with waxy white petals. Several bulb merchants offer these delights as well as the more usual hardy tulips and daffodils. More familiar perhaps is the plant still often called *Acidanthera bicolor*, although botanists have placed it in *Gladiolus* to which it bears some resemblance, so we must now call it *G. callianthus*. As the word callianthus means 'beautiful flower', this is an apt description of the plant. A sheaf of its elegantly arching white flowers, marked with maroon at their hearts (Fig. 13), and standing waist-high or taller in their autumn season, typifies the pleasure to be had from a conservatory. For here can be grown to perfection plants that would struggle, if they survived at all, in the open garden.

GROW YOUR OWN LEMONS

Visitors to the Mediterranean countries, or to the citrus-growing areas of Florida or California, can be heard admiring the lemon and orange trees with their fruit and sweetly perfumed flowers. This admiration is often tinged with regret that such things cannot be grown in frosty areas. However, in a conservatory from which frost is excluded you can easily grow the variety of lemon known as Meyer's. It bears its orange-blossom flowers and aromatic, juicy fruits from an early age. No lemon from a supermarket, thick of skin and sparse of juice, can compare with a freshly squeezed Meyer's from your own little tree.

Even plants such as lemons, which produce flowers at almost any season, cannot give us the unending source of fragrance of scented-leaved plants. Small wonder that the scented geraniums are such popular plants for house or conservatory. They are easy to grow, come in a variety of flavours, and are handsome in appearance. I use the word flavours advisedly, for some can be used to add aroma or perfume to cakes or milk puddings. Place a leaf or two of the rose-scented *Pelargonium capitatum* in the cake-tin before you pour in the mixture, or in a dish of rice pudding before it goes into the oven. Others are decidedly lemon-scented: *P. crispum, P. citriodorum* among them. 'Prince of Orange' is nearer to oranges than to lemons.

The incense aroma which we have already met in such plants as hoya, or *Humea elegans*, can be detected in the oak-leaved geranium, *P. quercifolium*. Others are nearer to the smell of pine or resin, and the furryleaved *P. tomentosum* smells of peppermint. They are so easy to increase from cuttings, and so good-tempered, that you could soon build up a collection. They mostly grow quickly and if kept indoors will need cutting back; the surplus growths can be used to make cuttings which can grow into plants to bed out, or tuck into tubs and containers on a patio, for next summer.

The flower-sellers' stalls in markets and city streets are often a good source of fragrant plants for conservatories. There you can buy the

Fig. 14 In a greenhouse, or in mild gardens, *Rhododendron* 'Fragrantissimum' lives up to its name with white, lily-shaped and lily-scented flowers.

broom, *Genista fragrans*, which bears its yellow flowers over a long season starting in winter. Little pots of jasmine or stephanotis, trained on wires into a hoop; pots of hyacinths in bud, to enjoy this year indoors and in years to come outside; the oriental lily or the Easter lily, *L. longiflorum*, with its fragrant white trumpets; little plants of the new race of fragrant *Cyclamen persicum*: all these can be acquired quite inexpensively.

To keep them in good health year after year, you should be prepared to feed them regularly, to keep them properly watered of course, and to repot them as needed. Many of these plants insist on water that is free of calcium, so it is worth saving rain water if you live in a hard-water area where kettles fur up and pipes get clogged. However, in an emergency, even hard tap water is better than no water at all. If a plant such as a rhododendron (Fig. 14) or a stephanotis turns yellowish from too much lime, this can be readily corrected by applying Sequestrene. Remember, too, that the flower buds of many plants are initiated long before they appear, and that a shortage of water at this stage may mean no flowers next season. No plant should be kept sopping wet while dormant or semi-dormant, and none likes to stand in water at any time. More plants in pots are killed by overwatering than by underwatering. In the constrictions of a pot or container the roots have no escape from sodden soil.

APPENDICES

PLANT TABLES

Trees with fragrant flowers

Trees with aromatic bark, wood or leaves

Shrubs with fragrant flowers

Shrubs with aromatic foliage

Climbers with fragrant flowers

Herbaceous plants with fragrant flowers

Herbaceous plants with aromatic foliage

Annuals and biennials with fragrant flowers

Bulbs, corms etc with fragrant flowers

EXPLANATION OF SIZES IN PLANT TABLES:

Trees:
    Small: 4.5–9 m (15–30 ft)
    Medium: 10–18 m (35–60 ft)
    Large: over 18 m (60 ft)

Shrubs:
    Dwarf: 30–60 cm (1–2 ft)
    Small: 1–1.5 m (3–5 ft)
    Medium: 1.5–3 m (5–10 ft)
    Large: over 3 m (10 ft)

Herbaceous Plants and Bulbs:
    Dwarf: under 30 cm (1 ft)
    Small: 30–60 cm (1–2 ft)
    Medium: 0.6–1.2 m (2–4 ft)
    Tall: over 1.2 m (4 ft), of narrow outline
    Large: over 1.2 m (4 ft), of bulky outline

TREES WITH FRAGRANT FLOWERS

Name	Flower Colour	Season	Fragrance	Plant Size	Other features
Acacia baileyana (mimosa)	Yellow	Winter	Mimosa	Small	Needs greenhouse protection in frosty areas
A. dealbata (mimosa)	Yellow	Winter	Mimosa	Small	Needs greenhouse protection in frosty areas
Aesculus hippocastanum (horse chestnut)	White	Spring		Large	
Cladrastis lutea (yellowwood)	White	Summer		Medium	
Eucryphia × intermedia 'Rostrevor'	White	Late summer	Delicate	Small	Evergreen; not for very cold areas. Narrow columnar habit
E. lucida	White	Late summer	Delicate	Small	Evergreen; not for very cold areas. Narrow columnar habit
Fraxinus mariesii (manna ash)	Cream	Summer		Small	
F. ornus	Cream	Summer		Medium	
Laburnum alpinum	Yellow	Early summer		Small	Flowers after 'Vossii'
L. × watereri 'Vossii'	Yellow	Late spring	Freesia-like	Small	Long flower tresses, fewer poisonous seeds
Ligustrum lucidum (privet)	White	Late summer		Small	Evergreen; handsome shiny foliage
Magnolia delavayi	Cream	Late summer			Large handsome evergreen leaves. Size depends on situation; not for cold areas. Can become large
M. grandiflora	Cream	Late summer	Lemon	Medium	Glossy evergreen foliage. Size depends on situation. Best in milder areas, but hardier than M. delavayi

Name	Flower Colour	Season	Fragrance	Plant Size	Other features
M. hypoleuca	Cream	Summer		Medium	
M. kobus	White	Spring	Delicate	Small	
M. × loebneri & cvs.	White	Spring		Small	'Merrill' is especially good cv.
M. salicifolia (willow-leaved magnolia)	White	Spring	Orange-blossom	Small	Leaves and bark aromatic (lemon/aniseed)
M. sprengeri 'Diva'	Pink	Spring		Small	
Malus angustifolia (crab)	Salmon pink	Spring	Violets	Small	
M. baccata (Siberian crab)	White	Spring	Apple-blossom	Small	Yellow or red fruits in autumn
M. coronaria 'Charlottae'	Shell-pink	Spring	Violets	Small	Semi-double blossom. Autumn colour
M. floribunda	Pink/white	Spring	Apple-blossom	Small	Cherry-red buds
M. 'Hillieri'	Rich pink	Spring		Small	Crimson buds
M. 'Hopa'	Wine-red	Spring		Small	Purple foliage
M. hupehensis	Pink/white	Spring		Small	
M. ioensis	White/pink	Spring		Small	Dislikes chalk soil
M. 'Profusion'	Claret-red	Spring		Small	Purple foliage
M. spectabilis 'Albiplena'	White	Spring	Violets	Small	Upright habit
Prunus conradinae	Blush	Early spring		Small	Needs shelter
P. mahaleb (St Lucie cherry)	White	Late spring		Small	

	Colour	Season		Size	Notes
P. mume (Japanese apricot)	Pink	Early spring	Almonds	Small	
P. mume 'Beni-shi-don'	Rich pink	Early spring	Hyacinths	Small	
P. pseudocerasus 'Cantabrigiensis'	Pink	Early spring		Small	
P. speciosa	White	Early spring		Medium	
P. 'Wadai'	Pale pink	Early spring	Peaches	Small	Deep pink buds
P. × yedoensis	Blush	Early spring	Almond	Small	Arching branches. Rare var. 'Ivensii' is white-flowered
Prunus, Japanese cherries	White/blush/pink	Late spring		Small	Varieties 'Amanogawa' (pink, columnar habit); Jo-nioi' (white, spreading, almond-scented); 'Shirotae' (white; horizontal branches); 'Taki-nioi' (white, honey-scented); 'Washi-no-o' (white, early-flowering) are a few fragrant varieties.
Robinia pseudoacacia (false acacia)	White	Summer		Large	
Styrax japonica (snowdrop tree)	White	Summer	Delicate	Small	
Tilia cordata (small-leaved lime)	Green-cream	Summer		Large	
T. × euchlora	Green-cream	Summer		Medium	Generally free of aphis
T. × europaea (common lime)	Green-cream	Summer		Large	
T. petiolaris (weeping silver lime)	Green-cream	Late summer		Large	Silvery undersides of leaves
T. platyphyllos (large-leaved lime)	Green-cream	Summer		Large	

TREES WITH AROMATIC BARK, WOOD OR LEAVES

Name	Plant Size	Aroma	Other features
Cercidiphyllum japonicum	Medium	Fallen leaves smell of hot toffee	Young foliage pinkish; autumn colour gold
Drimys winteri		Bark smells of wintergreen	Evergreen tree for mild areas; shrubby in colder areas. Scented white flowers in spring
Eucalyptus spp.	Large	Medicinal	Bristly white flowers in spring. Most can be cut back to remain shrubby; fast-growing, not for coldest areas
Juglans spp. (walnut)	Large	Aromatic leaves especially in autumn	
Liquidambar styraciflua	Medium	Botanical name derives from the sweet gum the tree emits	Brilliant autumn colour from maple-like leaves
Magnolia salicifolia (willow-leaved magnolia)	Small	Bark and foliage smell of aniseed or lemon	Fragrant flowers (see list above)
Populus × acuminata	Large	Balsam	
P. balsamifera (balsam poplar)	Large	Balsam	
P. × candicans	Large	Balsam	Variety 'Aurora' has foliage variegated pink, cream and green
P. trichocarpa	Very large	Balsam	
Umbellularia californica	Small	Pungent and spicy	Evergreen relative of bay laurel; yellow-green flowers in spring
Conifers, most: e.g. *Abies balsamea* (balsam fir)		Balsam	
Thuya plicata		Peardrops	

SHRUBS WITH FRAGRANT FLOWERS

Name	Flower Colour	Season	Fragrance	Plant Size	Other features
Abelia chinensis	Blush	Late summer		Small	
Azara microphylla	Yellow	Winter	Vanilla custard	Medium	Neat evergreen foliage. Makes small tree in mild areas; wall shrub in cold gardens
Berberis buxifolia	Yellow	Spring	Honey	Small	
B. sargentiana	Yellow	Spring	Honey	Medium	Evergreen
Buddleia asiatica	White	Winter	Sweet	Medium	Shelter; conservatory in cold areas
B. auriculata	Cream	Winter	Strong and sweet	Medium	Shelter; conservatory in cold areas
B. davidii & cvs. (butterfly bush)	Various	Late summer	Honey	Medium	Many colours of common butterfly bush – white, lilac, mauve, purple, violet
B. fallowiana	Lilac or white	Late summer	Honey	Medium	Good grey foliage. Less hardy than B. davidii
B. globosa	Orange	Early summer	Honey	Large	Flowers in rounded heads
B. 'Lochinch'	Lilac	Late summer	Honey	Large	Good silvery foliage, stout flower spikes
B. madagascariensis	Orange	Winter	Honey	Large	Conservatory except in mildest areas with no frost
B. × weyeriana	Buff-orange	Summer	Honey	Large	
Camellia sasanqua	White/pink/crimson	Winter		Medium	Evergreen foliage. 'Narumi-gata' is white, very sweetly perfumed
Cassinia fulvida	Whitish	Summer	Honey	Small	Old-gold foliage, evergreen
Chimonanthus praecox (wintersweet)	Translucent, or yellow	Winter	Very sweet	Large	Variety 'Luteus' is good clear yellow and just as sweetly scented as type

Name	Flower Colour	Season	Fragrance	Plant Size	Other features
Choisya ternata (Mexican orange-blossom)	White	Late spring	Orange-blossom	Medium	Glossy evergreen, aromatic foliage
Citrus spp. (lemon, orange)	White		Orange-blossom	Medium	Varieties of orange and lemon; need greenhouse protection in areas where frosts occur. May flower at almost any season. Variety 'Meyer's Lemon' very good for conservatories
Clerodendrum bungei	Rosy-crimson	Late summer	Sweet	Medium	Will behave like herbaceous plant in cold areas. Foliage smells of burnt rubber
C. trichotomum	Crimson/white	Late summer	Very sweet	Large	White petals drop and are followed by blue fruits in maroon calyces
Clethra alnifolia (sweet pepper bush)	White	Late summer		Medium	Lime-free soil only
Cornus mas (cornelian cherry)	Yellow	Winter	Sharp	Medium	
Corokia virgata	Yellow	Summer	Cocoa	Medium	Twiggy shrub with grey foliage, orange berries
Coronilla glauca	Yellow	Spring		Small	Pretty bluish foliage. Frost protection in cold areas
C. valentina	Yellow	Winter/spring	Ripe peaches	Dwarf	Like smaller version of above
Corylopsis spp.	Yellow	Early spring	Cowslips	Medium	*C. pauciflora* has largest individual flowers. Others, e.g. *C. veitchiana*, *C. willmottiae*, have smaller flowers in larger clusters
Cytisus battandieri (pineapple broom)	Yellow	Summer	Pineapple	Medium	Silvery foliage

Name	Flower colour	Season	Scent	Size	Notes
C. × praecox (Warminster broom)	Cream	Late spring	Heavy	Small	
Daphne spp.	Pink, or white/purple	Winter or spring	Very sweet	Small or medium	D. mezereum (white or purple flowers, winter); D. odora 'Aureomarginata' (purple and white flowers, late winter); D. cneorum (late spring, rich pink, spreading habit) and others
Deutzia 'Avalanche'	White	Summer		Medium	
D. compacta	White	Summer	Hawthorn	Small	Variety 'Lavender Time' has lilac flowers
D. × elegantissima	Pink	Summer		Medium	'Rosealind' is good rich-coloured kind
Elaeagnus × ebbingei	Buff	Late autumn		Large	Variegated kinds 'Limelight' and 'Gilt Edge' are very bright especially in winter
E. macrophylla	Buff	Late autumn		Large	Large silvered leaves
Erica arborea (tree heath)	White	Late winter	Honey	Medium	E. arborea 'Alpina' is a compact form
Eupatorium weinmannianum	White	Late summer	Sharp, spicy	Medium	Protect from frost
Freylinia lanceolata	Yellow	Winter		Small	Narrow evergreen leaves. Protect from frost
Genista cinerea (broom)	Yellow	Summer	Bean field	Large	G. virgata is similar
G. fragrans	Yellow	Spring		Small	Frost-tender
Hamamelis mollis (witch hazel)	Yellow	Winter	Spicy and sweet	Medium/ large	'Pallida' is paler yellow. 'Coombe Wood' is especially fragrant
H. 'Zuccariniana'	Yellow	Late winter	Sharp and spicy	Medium/ large	
Hebe speciosa & hybds.	Various	Summer	Very sweet	Small	Lilac, violet, purple, crimson, pink kinds. All frost tender. 'Midsummer Beauty' is hardier

Name	Flower Colour	Season	Fragrance	Plant Size	Other features
Ligustrum quihoui	White	Autumn		Medium	Elegant species of privet
Lonicera fragrantissima (shrubby honeysuckle)	Cream	Winter	Honeysuckle	Medium	Small flowers, intense sweet scent
L. × purpusii	Cream	Winter	Honeysuckle	Medium	Flowers slightly larger
L. standishii	Cream	Winter	Honeysuckle	Medium	Small flowers
L. syringantha	Lilac	Early summer	Honeysuckle	Small	
Lupinus arboreus (tree lupin)	Yellow	Early summer	Bean field	Medium	Very fast-growing. Easy from seed
Magnolia denudata (yulan)	White	Early spring		Medium	
M. sieboldii	White	Summer		Large	
M. sinensis	White	Summer	Lemon	Large	
M. × watsonii	Cream	Summer	Orange-blossom and lily	Large	
M. wilsonii	White	Summer		Large	
Mahonia japonica	Yellow	Winter	Lily-of-the-valley	Medium	Bold evergreen foliage
Myrtus communis (common myrtle)	White	Late summer		Medium	Evergreen. Shelter in cold areas. Aromatic foliage
M. luma	White	Late summer		Medium	Evergreen. Makes small tree in mild areas, with beautiful suede-textured cinnamon bark
Osmanthus × burkwoodii	White	Early spring	Very sweet	Medium	Dark evergreen foliage
O. decorus	White	Early spring		Medium	Handsome evergreen foliage. Formerly called *Phillyrea decora*

Name	Colour	Season	Scent	Size	Notes
O. delavayi	White	Early spring	Very sweet	Medium	Evergreen, neat foliage
O. heterophyllus	White	Autumn		Medium	Evergreen, holly-like foliage
Osmaronia cerasiformis	Cream	Early spring	Almond	Medium	Resembles flowering currant
Philadelphus coronarius & cvs. (mock orange)	Cream	Summer	Orange-blossom	Medium/large	*P. c.* 'Aureus' has handsome lime-yellow foliage; *P. c.* 'Bowles's Variety' is variegated white/green
P. delavayi	White	Summer	Orange-blossom	Large	
P. microphyllus	White	Summer	Orange-blossom	Small	
P. 'Belle Etoile'	White	Summer	Pineapple	Medium	
P. 'Manteau d'Hermine'	White	Summer	Orange-blossom	Small	
P. 'Sybille'	White	Summer	Orange-blossom	Small	Many other varieties, most sweetly scented
Pittosporum tenuifolium	Maroon	Spring	Chocolate	Large	Wavy-edged evergreen foliage. Shelter from frost
Rhododendron auriculatum	White	Summer	Very sweet	Large	Lime-free soil only
R. decorum	White or shell-pink	Spring		Medium	Lime-free soil only
R. discolor	White	Summer		Large	Lime-free soil only
R. fortunei	Lilac-pink	Late spring	Lily	Large	Lime-free soil only. Parent of *R.* 'Loderi' – several cvs., pink or white, all very fragrant
R. griffithianum	White	Late spring		Large	Lime-free soil only
R. johnstoneanum	White/cream	Late spring	Lily	Medium	Lime-free soil only. Shelter from frost
R. luteum (honeysuckle azalea)	Yellow	Late spring	Honeysuckle	Medium/large	Lime-free soil only

Name	Flower Colour	Season	Fragrance	Plant Size	Other features
Rhododendron hybrids: 'Argosy'	White	Summer	Very sweet	Large	Lime-free soil only
'Fragrantissimum'	White	Late spring	Lily	Medium	Shiny dark foliage. Easy from cuttings. Protect from frost. Lime-free soil only
'Polar Bear'	White	Late summer	Lily	Large	Lime-free soil only
Rhododendron: Azalea hybrids 'Daviesii'	White	Spring	Honeysuckle	Medium	Lime-free soil only
'Narcissiflorum'	Yellow	Spring	Honeysuckle	Medium	Lime-free soil only. Other Ghent and Occidentale azaleas also fragrant
Ribes alpinum (alpine currant)		Early spring		Small	
R. odoratum	Yellow	Early spring	Cloves	Medium	Rich autumn colour
Romneya coulteri (tree poppy)	White	Summer	Scented soap	Medium	Bluish foliage, running roots. Hard to establish, harder to eradicate. Behaves as a herbaceous plant in cold areas
R. trichocalyx	White	Summer	Scented soap	Medium	Similar to above. Both have wide flowers enhanced by golden stamens
Salix triandra (willow)	Yellow	Spring	Almond	Large	Flowers mimosa-like
Sarcococca spp.	Blush–white	Winter	Honey	Small	Evergreen low-growing shrubs with narrow foliage
Skimmia japonica 'Fragrans'	White	Spring	Lily-of-the-valley	Small/medium	Evergreen. Deep pink buds through winter
S.j. 'Rubella'	White	Spring	Lily-of-the-valley	Small/medium	Evergreen. Crimson buds through winter
Spartium japonicum (Spanish broom)	Yellow	Summer	Almond	Medium	Almost leafless green stems

Name	Colour	Season	Scent	Size	Notes
Syringa × chinensis (Rouen lilac)	Lilac	Spring	Lilac	Large	
S. microphylla 'Superba'	Pink	Spring and autumn	Lilac	Small	Neat foliage
S. × persica (Persian lilac)	Lilac or white	Spring	Lilac	Medium	
S. sweginzowii	Pale pink	Spring	Lilac	Medium	Most graceful of all lilacs in flower
S. velutina 'Palibin'	Lilac	Spring	Lilac	Small/medium	Neat foliage. Slow-growing but ultimately too big for rock gardens though often planted on them
S. vulgaris cvs. (common lilac)	Various	Spring	Lilac	Medium/large	Colours range from white through lilac, mauve to dark purple. Also a primrose variety
Viburnum × bodnantense	Blush	Winter	Almond	Large	'Deben' is nearer white, 'Dawn' has deep pink buds
V. × burkwoodii	White	Early spring	Carnation	Medium	Shiny evergreen foliage
V. × carlcephalum	White	Spring	Carnation	Medium	Deciduous; larger heads of flower than its parent V. carlesii
V. carlesii	White or pink	Spring	Carnation	Medium	'Aurora' and 'Charis' have pink flowers
V. farreri	Blush	Winter	Almond	Medium	Formerly called V. fragrans
V. foetens	White	Winter	Almond	Medium	
V. grandiflorum	Blush	Winter	Almond	Medium	
V. × juddii	Blush	Spring	Carnation	Medium	Newer kinds: 'Anne Russell', 'Fulbrook', 'Park Farm Hybrid'

SHRUBS WITH AROMATIC FOLIAGE

Name	Plant Size	Aroma	Other features
Aloysia triphylla (lemon verbena)	Medium	Foliage strongly fresh-lemon scented	Mauve flowers in summer. Protect against frost
Artemisia arborescens	Medium	Tangy	Very silvery foliage. Frost-tender
A. abrotanum (lad's love)	Small	Musty aroma	Feathery grey-green foliage
Caryopteris × *clandonensis*	Small	Sharply aromatic, hints of turpentine	Blue flowers in late summer set off by grey foliage
Cistus × *aguilari* (sun rose)	Medium	Sticky resinous foliage	White flowers all summer
C. × *cyprius*	Medium	Resin	White flowers all summer
C. ladanifer (gum cistus)	Medium	Resin	White flowers all summer
C. palhinhae	Medium	Glossy resinous sticky foliage	White flowers all summer
C. × *purpureus*	Small	Resinous foliage	Deep pink flowers in summer
Drimys lanceolata	Medium	Wintergreen	Evergreen. White spring flowers
Elsholtzia stauntonii	Medium	Mint	Mauve flowers in summer
Gaultheria procumbens	Dwarf	Wintergreen	Spreading low evergreen; white bell-shaped flowers in late spring followed by red fruits
Hebe cupressoides	Small	Cypress-like blue-grey foliage smelling of pencil-sharpenings	Pale blue flowers in summer
Helichrysum italicum (curry plant)	Small	Silvery needle-like foliage smelling of cheap curry powder	Yellow flowers in summer
H. plicatum	Small	Curry	Longer needles, otherwise similar to above
Hypericum 'Hidcote'	Medium	Like cough sweets	Yellow flowers with showy stamens in summer

Lavandula spica (lavender)	Small	Lavender	Both grey foliage and pale mauve flower spikes aromatic
Olearia ilicifolia (daisy bush)	Medium	Musk	Holly-like foliage; white daisy-like flowers in summer
O. mollis	Small	Musk	Small grey leaves
O. moschata	Small	Musk	Small woolly grey leaves
Osmanthus ledifolius	Small	Whole plant smells of stewed prunes	White flowers in summer
Perovskia spp. (Russian sage)	Small	Turpentine-scented leaves	Spikes of lilac blue flowers in summer
Prostanthera spp. (Australian mint bush)	Small	Foliage smells a little like mint	Pink, white or lilac flowers in spring. Protect from frost
Rhododendron cinnabarinum	Medium	Attractive glaucous foliage, saddle-soap aroma	Flowers waxy bells in soft red. Lime-free soil only
R. glaucophyllum	Small	Strongly saddle-soap	Pink flowers, foliage white below. Lime-free soil only
R. oreotrephes	Medium	Aroma similar to above	Glaucous foliage and lilac flowers. Lime-free soil only
R. saluenense	Small	Saddle soap	Rose-purple flowers
Rosa multibracteata	Large	Saddle soap	Sweetly scented lilac pink flowers
R. primula (incense rose)	Medium	Ferny foliage smells of incense, especially when young	Early single, yellow flowers
R. rubiginosa (sweet briar)	Large	Foliage smells of apples	Sweet-scented pink blooms
Rosmarinus officinalis (rosemary)	Small	Rosemary	Evergreen. Blue flowers in spring
Ruta graveolens (rue)	Small	Very pungent blue-grey foliage	Yellow summer flowers. Best form is 'Jackman's Blue'
Salvia grahamii	Small	Foliage smells of blackcurrants	Red flowers in summer. Protect from frost

Name	Plant Size	Aroma	Other features
S. neurepia	Small	Foliage smells of blackcurrants	Scarlet flowers. Protect from frost
S. rutilans (pineapple sage)	Small	Foliage smells of pineapple	Scarlet flowers in late summer. Protect from frost
Santolina spp. (cotton lavender)	Small/ dwarf	Variable, usually pungent	Most have silvery foliage with yellow button flowers in summer
Skimmia laureola	Small		Evergreen. Green flowers smelling of lily-of-the-valley
Thymus spp. (thyme)	Dwarf	Most have thyme-scented foliage; T. herba-barona is caraway-scented, T. citriodorus has lemon overtones	Lilac flowers in summer

CLIMBERS WITH FRAGRANT FLOWERS

Name	Flower Colour	Season	Fragrance	Plant Size	Other features
Clematis armandii	Cream	Spring	Almond	Vigorous	Variety 'Snowdrift', pure white; 'Apple Blossom', pink. Evergreen foliage. Shelter
C. cirrhosa balearica	Cream, freckled	Winter	Lemon	Medium	Shelter. Ferny evergreen foliage
C. flammula	White	Late summer	Hawthorn	Vigorous	
C. montana	White or pink	Spring	Vanilla	Vigorous	Some varieties fragrant, others not (see text)
C. rehderiana	Yellow	Autumn	Cowslip	Vigorous	C. veitchiana is similar
Holboellia latifolia	Whitish	Spring	Very sweet	Vigorous	Evergreen. Shelter
Humulus lupulus (hop)	Green	Late summer		Vigorous	Perennial. Dies down each year. Variety 'Aureus', lime-yellow foliage

Name	Colour	Season	Fragrance	Vigour	Notes
Jasminum azoricum (jasmine)	White	Summer	Jasmine	Medium	Conservatory protection except in frost-free areas
J. officinale (summer jasmine)	White	Summer	Jasmine	Vigorous	
J. polyanthum	White	Spring	Jasmine	Medium	Shelter except in mild areas, or grow as house plant. Some forms have pink buds
J. × stephanense	Pink	Summer	Jasmine	Vigorous	
Lonicera × americana (honeysuckle)	Pink/cream	Summer	Honeysuckle	Vigorous	
L. caprifolium	Cream	Late spring	Honeysuckle	Vigorous	
L. etrusca	Cream	Summer	Honeysuckle	Vigorous	
L. × heckrotii 'Gold Flame'	Orange-yellow	Summer	Honeysuckle	Vigorous	Brightest in flower of the scented kinds
L. japonica (Japanese honeysuckle)	Cream	Summer	Honeysuckle	Vigorous	
L. periclymenum & cvs. (woodbine)	Purple/cream	Summer	Honeysuckle	Vigorous	
Mandevilla suaveolens (Chilean jasmine)	White	Summer/autumn	Sweet	Vigorous	Shelter except in mild areas
Stauntonia hexaphylla	Whitish	Spring	Very sweet	Vigorous	Shelter except in mild areas
Trachelospermum asiaticum	Cream	Late summer	Very sweet	Medium	Shelter except in mild areas
T. jasminoides	White	Late summer	Very sweet	Medium	Shelter except in mild areas. 'Variegatum' with pink/green/cream leaves seems hardier
Wattakaka sinensis	White	Late summer	Very sweet	Medium	Shelter except in mild areas
Wisteria sinensis	Lilac	Late spring	Bean field	Vigorous	Other species of wisteria are generally less fragrant

HERBACEOUS PLANTS WITH FRAGRANT FLOWERS

Name	Flower Colour	Season	Fragrance	Plant Size	Other features
Cestrum parqui	Yellow	Late summer	Very sweet	Large	Night-fragrant only. Shrubby in mild areas
Chrysanthemum	Various	Autumn	Tangy	Small/medium/tall	
Clematis heracleifolia	Blue	Summer	Hair-oil	Medium	
Convallaria majalis (lily-of-the-valley)	White	Spring	Lily-of-the-valley	Small	
Cosmos atrosanguineus (chocolate plant)	Maroon	Summer	Cocoa	Medium	
Dahlia	Various	Late summer	Tangy	Small/medium	
Delphinium wellbyi	Pale blue–green	Summer		Medium	Protect from frost
Dianthus (pinks and carnations)	White/pink/crimson	Summer	Clove	Small	
Filipendula ulmaria (meadowsweet)	White	Early summer		Medium	
Helleborus lividus (hellebore)	Dove grey	Early spring	Sweet	Medium	Shelter except in mild areas
H. foetidus (stinking hellebore)	Green	Winter	Sweet	Medium	Some kinds only are scented
Hemerocallis citrina (day lily)	Yellow	Summer	Lily	Medium	
H. dumortieri	Yellow	Early summer	Lily	Small/medium	
H. flava (lemon lily)	Yellow	Early summer	Lily	Medium	

Name	Colour	Season	Scent	Size	Notes
H. middendorffiana	Yellow	Summer	Lily	Medium	
H. multiflora	Yellow	Summer	Lily	Medium	
H. named kinds	Yellow	Summer	Lily	Medium	Most yellow-flowered kinds are scented, e.g. 'Golden Chimes', 'Hyperion', 'Marion Vaughn'
Hesperis matronalis (sweet rocket)	White/lilac	Late spring	Clove	Medium	Sows itself
Hosta 'Honeybells'	Lilac-white	Summer	Lily	Medium	
H. plantaginea 'Grandiflora'	White	Late summer	Lily	Medium	
H. 'Royal Standard'	White	Summer	Lily	Medium	
Iris florentina	Grey-white	Early summer		Medium	Roots also fragrant: when dried and ground they make orris root powder, used in pot pourri
I. germanica (flag iris)	Purple	Early summer		Medium	
I. graminea (plum tart iris)	Purple	Summer	Stewed plums	Small	
I. hoogiana	Lavender	Early summer		Medium	
I. pallida dalmatica	Lavender	Early summer	Orange-blossom	Medium	
I. unguicularis	Lavender	Winter		Medium	
Lupinus polyphyllus (Lupin)	Various	Early summer	Beanfield	Medium/large	Russell lupins and newer strains
Mirabilis jalapa (marvel of Peru)	Various	Summer		Medium/large	Frost-tender
Paeonia (peony)	White/pink/crimson	Summer		Medium	Some Chinese paeonies are fragrant

Name	Flower Colour	Season	Fragrance	Plant Size	Other features
Phlox, border cvs.	Various	Late summer	Warm, peppery	Medium/large	
P. maculata & cvs.	White/lilac	Late summer	Warm, peppery	Large	
Primula alpicola	White/primrose/lilac	Early summer	Cowslip	Medium	Moist soil
P. florindae (Himalayan cowslip)	Primrose/red	Summer	Cowslip	Tall	Yellow shades are prettiest; where red and yellow are grown together intermediate-coloured seedlings, orange and copper, will appear
P. secundiflora	Maroon	Early summer	Cowslip	Medium	
P. sikkimensis	Primrose	Early summer	Cowslip	Medium	Resembles a smaller *P. florindae*
Smilacina racemosa	White	Spring	Sweet	Medium	Foliage like Solomon's seal, flowers fluffy sprays
Verbena bonariensis	Purple	Summer	Sweet	Tall	
V. corymbosa	Purple	Summer	Sweet	Medium	Very vigorous spreading growth
Viola odorata (violet)	Violet/white/pink	Spring	Violet	Dwarf	Parma violets, with larger double flowers, need frame protection in cold areas
Yucca filamentosa	White	Summer		Large	Most fragrant in the evening

HERBACEOUS PLANTS WITH AROMATIC FOLIAGE

Name	Plant Size	Aroma	Other features
Acorus calamus (sweet rush)	Large	Crushed foliage smells of cinnamon	
Anthemis nobilis (chamomile)	Small	Fresh green foliage smells strongly of apples	White daisy-like flowers in summer
Artemisia spp.	Medium/large	Tangy silver foliage	Dull buff flowers in summer
Calamintha grandiflora	Small	Tangy-fresh with hints of mint	Pink flowers in summer
C. nepetoides	Small		Foliage as above but with lilac flowers
Dictamnus albus (burning bush)	Medium	Lemony	White or lilac flowers in early summer. Leaves give off an aromatic oil; will light on hot still days
Dracocephalum spp.	Medium	Similar to *Nepeta*	
Elsholtzia stauntonii	Large	Minty fragrance	Mauve flowers in autumn
Foeniculum vulgare (fennel)	Tall	Aniseed	Feathery foliage with umbels of yellow flowers in summer
Geranium macrorrhizum	Small	Strongly aromatic geranium foliage	Good ground cover. Flowers in early summer in several shades of pink and purple, and white
Houttuynia cordata	Small	Leaves smell strongly of orange peel	White flowers in summer
Leontopodium aloysiodorum	Small	Leaves smell of lemon verbena	Flowers resemble edelweiss and appear in early summer
Melissa officinalis (lemon balm)	Medium	Leaves smell of rather synthetic lemon	White flowers in summer
Mentha pulegium (pennyroyal)	Small	Pungent minty smell	Mauve summer flowers
M. requienii (creeping mint)	Dwarf	Very strong peppermint smell	Other mints include 'ginger mint', 'spearmint', 'peppermint', 'eau de cologne mint', 'apple mint', etc.

Name	Plant Size	Description	Other features
Monarda didyma (bergamot)	Medium	Earl Grey tea	Whorls of shaggy pink, red or purple flowers in summer
Nepeta × faassenii	Medium	Related to catmint	Lilac flowers in summer. Aromatic foliage attractive to cats
Perovskia spp. (Russian sage)	Medium	Grey turpentine-smelling foliage	Spires of blue flowers in summer
Salvia candidissima	Medium	Sage	Yellow and white flowers in summer
Teucrium hyrcanum (germander)	Small	Herby	Purple flowers in summer

ANNUALS AND BIENNIALS WITH FRAGRANT FLOWERS

Name	Flower Colour	Season	Fragrance	Plant Size	Other features
Abronia arenaria (Californian sand verbena)	Yellow	Summer	Honeysuckle	Dwarf	
A. umbellata (sand verbena)	Rose pink	Summer	Honey	Dwarf	Especially fragrant at night
Alyssum maritimum (sweet alyssum)	White/pink/purple	Summer	Honey	Dwarf	
Asperula azurea setosa (blue woodruff)	Blue	Summer		Dwarf	
Centaurea moschata (sweet sultan)	Lilac/purple/white/yellow	Summer		Medium	

Plant	Colour	Season	Scent	Size	Notes
Cheiranthus cheiri (wallflower)	Various	Spring	Clove	Small	
Dianthus barbatus (sweet william)	Various	Summer	Clove	Small	
Erysimum capitatum	Cream	Spring	Clove	Small	Related to wallflowers. Shelter in colder gardens
Exacum affine	Mauve/white	Summer		Dwarf	
Heliotropium (cherry pie)	Violet	Summer	Cherry/almond	Small	Paler, old-fashioned kind, or old named kinds such as 'Lord Roberts', have more fragrance than modern, deeper-coloured kinds such as 'Marine'
Humea elegans (incense plant)	Brown	Summer	Incense	Tall	Dried flowers retain aroma
Iberis odorata (candytuft)	White/pinks	Summer		Dwarf	
Ionopsidium acaule	Lilac and white	Summer	Honey	Dwarf	
Lathyrus odoratus (sweet pea)	Various	Summer	Sweet pea	Dwarf to tall	
Limnanthes douglasii (poached-egg flower)	Yellow and white	Summer		Dwarf	Good bee plant
Lupinus hartwegii (annual lupin)	Blue	Summer	Bean field	Medium	
L. luteus	Yellow	Summer	Bean field	Medium	
L. mutabilis	Various	Summer	Bean field	Medium	
Matthiola bicornis (night-scented stock)	Buff	Summer	Very sweet	Small	
M. incana (stock)	Various	Spring/summer	Clove	Dwarf/small/medium	See text for different types

Name	Flower Colour	Season	Fragrance	Plant Size	Other features
Nicotiana affinis (tobacco flower)	White	Summer	Rich	Medium	N. alata 'Grandiflora' is also very sweet. Both best in the evening
N. sylvestris	White	Summer	Rich	Tall	Broad ground-covering rosettes of foliage
Oenothera biennis (evening primrose)	Yellow	Summer	Sweet	Medium	
Petunia	Various	Summer		Small	Blue-flowered kinds especially are fragrant in the evening
Reseda odorata (mignonette)	Reddish	Summer	Sweet	Small	The 'unimproved' kind has better fragrance than those with brighter coloured flowers
Scabiosa atropurpurea (sweet scabious)	Various	Summer	Honey	Small	Neat, 'pincushion' flowers in all shades of pink and purple, and white
Schizopetalum walkeri	White	Summer		Dwarf	Fringed petals
Tropaeolum majus (nasturtium)	Yellow/ orange/ red	Summer		Small/ medium	

BULBS, CORMS ETC. WITH FRAGRANT FLOWERS

Name	Flower Colour	Season	Fragrance	Plant Size	Other features
Amaryllis belladonna	Pink	Autumn	Ripe apricots	Medium	Not for cold areas. Maximum sun to flower well
Crinum spp.	Pink/ white	Summer	Lily	Tall	
Crocus chrysanthus	Various	Winter	Very sweet	Dwarf	
C. imperati	Purple	Winter		Dwarf	
Cyclamen persicum	White/ pink	Winter/ spring	Sweet	Dwarf	Wild species, and small-flowered cultivars of pale colour, have best fragrance. None from large-flowered or bright-coloured kinds
Freesia refracta	White/ primrose	Spring		Small	Some fragrance remains in coloured kinds, but very faint compared with *F. refracta*
Galanthus spp. (snowdrop)	White	Winter	Honey	Small	
Galtonia candicans (Cape hyacinth)	White	Summer		Tall	
Gladiolus callianthus	White	Autumn		Tall	Formerly called *Acidanthera bicolor*
G. tristis	Buff- yellow	Summer	Very sweet	Medium	Especially fragrant at night
Hedychium spp. (ginger lily)	White/ yellow/ orange	Late summer	Very sweet	Tall	*H. gardnerianum* (yellow) is most readily available and one of the most handsome. Protect from frost
Hymenocallis spp.	White/ yellow	Spring		Small/ medium	Protect from frost
Iris reticulata	Violet/ purple/ blue	Winter	Violet	Dwarf	

Name	Flower Colour	Season	Fragrance	Plant Size	Other features
Lilium (many) (lily)	White/crimson/yellow	Summer	Heavy and sweet	Medium	See text for names of good fragrant kinds
Muscari 'Heavenly Blue' (grape hyacinth)	Blue	Spring	Sweet	Small	Other kinds, e.g. *M. ambrosiacum, M. moschatum*, are rare, and desirable for their perfume
Narcissus jonquilla (jonquil)	Yellow	Spring	Sweet	Small	
N. poeticus	White	Spring	Very sweet	Small	The wild narcissus of alpine meadows. *N. poeticus recurvus* is the dainty late-flowering kind, 'Actaea', a broader-petalled named kind
N. triandrus	Cream	Spring		Dwarf	
Narcissus, named kinds	Various	Spring		Small	Especially sweet are 'Cheerfulness' (double cream), 'Yellow Cheerfulness', 'Geranium' (white and red) and many small-cupped kinds
Polianthes tuberosa (tuberose)	White		Extremely sweet		Greenhouse cultivation
Tulipa clusiana (lady tulip)	Red and white	Spring	Delicate	Small	
T. sylvestris	Yellow	Spring	Delicate	Small	

GLOSSARY OF BOTANICAL NAMES SUGGESTING FRAGRANCE

As well as all the possible English names indicating that a plant is fragrant – 'sweet', as in sweet pea, sweet william, sweet sultan, is a favourite – there are several botanical names that have been bestowed on plants for this same quality. Here are some of them:

Name	Meaning	Example
ambrosiacus/a/um	ambrosial	*Muscari ambrosiacum*
anisodorus/a/um	aniseed-smelling	*Primula anisodora*
aromaticus/a/um	aromatic	*Drimys aromatica*
balsamiferus/a/um	balsam-bearing	*Populus balsamifera*
citriodorus/a/um	lemon-smelling	*Lippia citriodora*
fragrans	fragrant	*Genista fragrans*
fragrantissimus/a/um	extremely fragrant	*Lonicera fragrantissima*
graveolens	strong-smelling, unpleasant-smelling	*Ruta graveolens*
moschatus/a/um	musk-smelling	*Centaurea moschata*
odoratissimus/a/um	very sweet-smelling	*Viburnum odoratissimum*
odoratus/a/um	sweet-smelling	*Reseda odorata*
odorus/a/um	sweet-smelling	*Daphne odora*
pungens	strong-smelling (can also mean sharp)	*Elaeagnus pungens*
suaveolens	sweet-smelling	*Datura suaveolens*
suavis	sweet	*Viola suavis*
suavissimus/a/um	extremely sweet	*Jasminum suavissimum*

BIBLIOGRAPHY

Bowles, E.A.
'Fragrance in the Garden'
Journal of the Royal Horticultural
Society, Vol. 78, pp. 87–95 (1953)

Genders, Roy
Scented Flora of the World
Robert Hale, 1977

Lloyd, Christopher
The Well-Tempered Garden
Collins, 1970

Rohde, E. Sinclair
The Scented Garden
Medici Society, 1931

Sanecki, Kay
Fragrant & Aromatic Plants
Wisley Handbook:
Royal Horticultural Society, 1985

Sanecki, Kay
The Fragrant Garden
Batsford, 1981

Taylor, Jane
Fragrant Gardens
Ward Lock, 1987

Thomas, G.S.
Climbing Roses Old & New
Dent, 1967

Thomas, G.S.
Shrub Roses of Today
Dent, 1974

Thomas, G.S.
The Old Shrub Roses
Dent, 1978

Thomas, G.S.
'Fragrance in the Garden'
Journal of the Royal Horticultural
Society, Vol. 88, pp. 288–294 and
342–349 (1963)

Verey, Rosemary
The Scented Garden
Michael Joseph, 1981

INDEX

Abelia chinensis, 73
Abies balsamea, 63,72
Abronia, 88
Acacia, 69
Acidanthera bicolor,
    65–66
Acorus calamus, 87
Aesculus hippocastanum,
    69
Aloysia triphylla, 12, 80
Alyssum maritimum, 22,
    88
Amaryllis belladonna, 9,
    91
Anthemis nobilis, 50, 87
Artemisia, 87
    abrotanum, 11, 49, 80
    arborescens, 80
Azalea see
    Rhododendron
Azara microphylla, 46, 73

Basil, 52
Berberis buxifolia, 73
    × ottawensis
        'Superba', 20
    sargentiana, 16, 41, 73
    thunbergii 'Rose
        Glow', 34
Buddleia, 41
    asiatica, 73
    auriculata, 73
    fallowiana, 73
    globosa, 73
    'Lochinch', 18, 73
    madagascariensis, 73
    × weyeriana, 19, 73

Calamintha, 87
Camellia, 11
    sasanqua, 73
Campanula
    persicifolia, 54
Caryopteris ×
    clandonensis, 49, 80
Cassinia fulvida, 73
Centaurea moschata, 88
Cercidiphyllum
    japonicum, 63, 72
Cestrum parqui, 38, 84
Cheiranthus cheiri, 19, 25,
    62, 89

Chimonanthus praecox, 8,
    45, 73
Choisya ternata, 13, 41,
    74
Chrysanthemum, 84
Citrus, 66, 74
Cladrastis lutea, 69
Clematis armandii, 82
    cirrhosa balearica, 82
    flammula, 82
    heracleifolia, 84
    montana, 33, 82
    'Mrs Cholmondely',
        34
    rehderiana, 82
Clerodendrum, 74
Clethra alnifolia, 11, 74
Convallaria majalis, 44,
    84
Cornus mas, 74
Corokia virgata, 74
Coronilla, 74
Corylopsis, 74
Cosmos atrosanguineus,
    20, 63, 84
Cotinus 'Royal
        Purple', 19
Crocosmia 'Solfatare', 19
Crocus chrysanthus, 16,
    19, 47, 91
    imperati, 91
Cyclamen persicum, 47,
    91
Cytisus battandieri, 74
    × praecox, 42, 52, 75

Dahlia, 84
Daphne, 75
    odora 'Aureo-
        marginata', 36
    pontica, 36
Datura suaveolens, 40
Delphinium wellbyi, 84
Deutzia, 75
Dianthus, 18, 44–45, 62,
    84
    barbatus, 24, 89
Dictamnus albus, 87
Digitalis grandiflora, 53
Dracocephalum, 87
Drimys lanceolata, 80
    winteri, 72

Elaeagnus × ebbingei, 75
    'Limelight', 16
    macrophylla, 75
Elscholzia stauntonii, 80,
    87
Erica arborea, 75
Erysimum capitatum, 62,
    89
    'Moonlight', 62
Eucalyptus, 72
Eucharis grandiflora,
    65
Eucryphia × intermedia
    'Rostrevor', 30, 69
    lucida, 69
Eupatorium
    weinmannianum, 75
Exacum affine, 89

Filipendula ulmaria, 84
Foeniculum vulgare, 19,
    87
Freesia refracta, 65, 91
Freylinia lanceolata, 75

Galanthus, 46–47, 91
Galtonia candicans, 91
Gardenia, 64
Gaultheria procumbens, 80
Genista cinerea, 75
    fragrans, 67, 75
Geranium 'Johnson's
        Blue', 59
    macrorrhizum, 41, 87
Gladiolus callianthus,
    66, 91
    tristis, 91

Hamamelis, 8
    japonica
        'Zuccariniana', 45,
        75
    mollis, 45, 75
Hebe cupressoides, 63, 80
    speciosa, 75
Hedychium gardnerianum,
    65, 91
Helianthemum 'Wisley
    Pink', 34
Helichrysum, 62
    italicum, 80
    plicatum, 80

Heliotropium, 89
Helleborus foetidus, 18, 84
    lividus, 84
Hemerocallis, 44
    citrina, 41, 84
    dumortieri, 84
    flava, 16, 84
    'Golden Chimes', 19
    middendorfiana, 85
    multiflora, 85
    var., 85
Hesperis matronalis, 37,
    85
Holboellia latifolia, 82
Hosta, 85
    sieboldiana 'Elegans',
        34, 56
Houttuynia cordata, 52,
    87
Hoya, 64
Humea elegans, 13, 66, 89
Humulus lupulus, 82
Hyacinthus, 13
Hymenocallis, 91
Hypericum 'Hidcote', 80

Iberis odorata, 89
Iris florentina, 85
    germanica, 85
    graminea, 44, 85
    hoogiana, 85
    pallida dalmatica, 18,
        55, 85
    reticulata, 91
    unguicularis, 46, 61, 85

Jasminum azoricum, 83
    officinale, 83
    polyanthum, 64, 83
    × stephanense, 83

Kniphofia, 19

Laburnum, 69
Lathyrus odoratus, 21–22,
    44, 89
Lavandula 'Hidcote', 49
    spica, 81
    stoechas, 49
Leontopodium
    aloysiodorum, 87

Ligustrum lucidum, 69
  quihoui, 76
Lilium, 12, 92
  candidum, 37–38
  longiflorum, 67
  regale, 18, 19, 34
  speciosum, 40, 64
  × testaceum, 19
Limnanthus douglasii, 89
Liquidambar styraciflua, 72
Lonicera, 9, 13, 34–35
  × americana, 83
  caprifolium, 83
  etrusca, 83
  fragrantissima, 76
  × heckrotii 'Gold Flame', 83
  japonica, 32, 83
  periclymenum, 19, 83
  × purpusii, 46, 76
  standishii, 76
  syringantha, 76
Lupinus arboreus, 13, 16, 76
  hartwegii, 25, 89
  luteus, 25, 89
  mutabilis, 25, 89

Magnolia, 11, 28–29
  delavayi, 69
  denudata, 28, 76
  grandiflora, 29, 69
  × highdownensis, 29
  hypoleuca, 70
  kobus, 70
  × loebneri, 28, 70
  salicifolia, 42, 70, 72
  sieboldii, 29, 76
  sinensis, 29, 76
  stellata, 28
  × watsonii, 76
  wilsonii, 29, 76
Mahonia japonica, 16, 76
Malus, 27, 70
Mandevilla suaveolens, 9, 83
Matthiola, 23–24
  bicornis, 12, 40, 89
  incana, 89
Melissa officinalis, 87
Mentha pulegium, 51, 87
  requienii, 51, 87
  rotundifolia 'Variegata', 52
Mirabilis jalapa, 38, 85
Monarda didyma, 51, 88
Muscari, 41
  'Heavenly Blue', 92

Myrtis communis, 12, 76
  luma, 76

Narcissus 'Actaea', 36
  jonquilla, 92
  poeticus, 92
  triandrus, 92
  var., 92
  'Yellow Cheerfulness', 16
Nepeta × faassenii, 51–52
Nicotiana, 12
  affinis, 38, 90
  sylvestris, 38, 90

Oenothera biennis, 90
  odorata, 38
Olearia, 81
Osmanthus × burkwoodii, 76
  decorus, 76
  delavayi, 77
  heterophyllus, 77
  ledifolius, 81
Osmaronia cerasiformis, 77

Paeonia, 85
Pelargonium, 66
Perovskia atriplicifolia, 49, 81, 88
Petunia, 12, 38–40, 90
Philadelphus, 13, 41
  'Beauclerk', 63
  'Belle Etoile', 18, 77
  coronarius, 16, 42, 77
  delavayi, 77
  microphyllus, 77
  'Sybille', 77
Phlox, 86
  maculata, 86
  'Mia Ruys', 38
Pittosporum tenuifolium, 77
Polianthes tuberosa, 65, 92
Populus × acuminata, 72
  balsamifera, 9, 30, 72
  × candicans, 30, 72
  trichocarpa, 72
Potentilla, 34
Primula, 86
Prostanthera, 81
Prunus, 71
  conradinae, 70
  'Jo-nioi', 27
  mahaleb, 70
  mume, 71
  pseudocerasus 'Cantabrigiensis', 71

speciosa, 71
  'Wadai', 71
  × yedoensis, 27, 71
Pyrus salicifolia 'Pendula', 28

Reseda odorata, 90
Rhododendron, 11
  'Argosy', 78
  auriculatum, 77
  cinnabarinum, 81
  'Daviesii', 78
  decorum, 77
  discolor, 77
  fortunei, 77
  glaucophyllum, 81
  griffithianum, 77
  johnstoneanum, 77
  luteum, 13, 16, 77
  oreotrephes, 81
  'Polar Bear', 78
  saluenense, 81
Ribes, 78
Robinia pseudoacacia 'Freesia', 20, 28, 71
Romneya, 78
Rosa, 13, 53–60
  alba, 54–56
  Bourbon, 56
  'Buff Beauty', 19
  burnet, 57
  centifolia, 54
  climbing. 30–34
  damask, 56
  'Frühlingsgold', 16, 20
  gallica, 57
  hybrid musk, 57–58
  'Louise Odier', 18
  'Madame Hardy', 37
  'Margaret Merrill', 37
  'Moonlight', 19
  moss, 53–54
  multibracteata, 58, 81
  primula, 58, 81
  'Reine des Violettes', 18
  rubiginosa, 9, 58, 81
  rugosa, 9, 20, 37, 57
  shrub, 56–60
  spinosissima, 56–57
  'Zéphyrine Drouhin', 13, 34
Rosmarinus officinalis, 81
Ruta graveolens, 34, 81

Salix triandra, 9, 78
Salvia candidissima, 88
  grahamii, 81
  lavandulifolia, 49

neurepia, 82
officinalis
  'Purpurascens', 18, 52
  rutilans, 12–13, 82
Santolina, 82
  incana, 49
  neapolitana, 49
Sarcococca, 46, 78
Scabiosa atropurpurea, 90
Schizopetalum walkeri, 62, 90
Skimmia japonica, 78
  laureola, 82
Smilacina racemosa, 86
Spartium japonicum, 78
Stauntonia hexaphylla, 83
Stephanotis, 64
Styrax japonica, 71
Syringa, 42
  × chinensis, 79
  × persica, 79
  sweginzowii, 79
  velutina 'Palibin', 79
  vulgaris, 79

Thuya, 63
  plicata, 72
Thymus herba-barona, 50
  serpyllum, 49
Tilia, 4, 71
Trachelospermum, 83
Tropaeolum majus, 24, 90
Tulipa clusiana, 92
  'De Wet', 20
  'Orange Parrot', 20
  sylvestris, 92

Umbellularia californica, 9, 72
Verbena, 23
  bonariensis, 18, 40, 86
  corymbosa, 86
  venosa, 23
Viburnum × bodnantense, 46, 79
  × burkwoodii, 36, 79
  × carlcephalum, 79
  carlesii, 36, 79
  farreri, 46, 79
  foetens, 79
  grandiflorum, 79
  × juddii, 79
  tinus, 46
Viola odorata, 86

Wattakaka sinensis, 46, 83
Wisteria sinensis, 83
Yucca filamentosa, 86